Water and Health: Advancing Safe Drinking Water, Sanitation, Hygiene, Climate Change Resilience, Public Health, and Sustainable Development

Copyright

Water and Health: Advancing Safe Drinking Water, Sanitation, Hygiene, Climate Change Resilience, Public Health, and Sustainable Development

© 2025 Robert C. Brears

ISBN (eBook): 978-1-991368-39-3

ISBN (Paperback): 978-1-991368-40-9

Published by Global Climate Solutions

First Edition, 2025

Cover design and interior layout by Global Climate Solutions

Table of Contents

Introduction

Chapter 1: The Fundamental Role of Water in Human Health

Chapter 2: Water Quality and Human Health Risks

Chapter 3: Sanitation, Hygiene, and Disease Prevention

Chapter 4: Water-Related Vector-Borne and Parasitic Diseases

Chapter 5: Water Scarcity, Food Security, and Nutrition

Chapter 6: Climate Change, Water Systems, and Health Impacts

Chapter 7: Water Infrastructure and Health System Resilience

Chapter 8: Socioeconomic Inequalities, Water Access, and Health

Chapter 9: Governance, Policy, and Integrated Approaches

Conclusion

Introduction

Water is the essence of life, indispensable for sustaining human health and well-being. It plays a fundamental role in every aspect of physiological functioning, from regulating body temperature and transporting nutrients to removing waste products and maintaining cellular homeostasis. Beyond its biological necessity, water underpins the foundations of public health by enabling sanitation, hygiene, and safe food preparation. Access to clean and sufficient water is a critical determinant of health outcomes, influencing disease prevention, child survival, and overall quality of life. Yet despite its importance, billions of people worldwide still lack reliable access to safe drinking water, while waterborne diseases remain a leading cause of illness and death, especially among children in low- and middle-income countries.

The quality and safety of water are as crucial as its availability. Contaminated water sources can transmit a wide range of pathogens, including bacteria, viruses, and parasites, which cause diarrheal diseases, cholera, dysentery, typhoid, and other infections. Chemical pollutants, such as arsenic, lead, and nitrates, pose additional risks, contributing to chronic illnesses including cancer, developmental disorders, and reproductive health problems. Exposure to these hazards disproportionately affects vulnerable populations, particularly those living in poverty or in areas with inadequate infrastructure and weak regulatory oversight. Safe water is thus both a health necessity and a matter of environmental justice, requiring careful management to protect public health.

Water scarcity adds another layer of complexity, undermining food security, nutrition, and hygiene practices. In arid and drought-prone regions, insufficient water limits agricultural production, reduces dietary diversity, and contributes to malnutrition. Scarcity also forces communities to rely on unsafe water sources, increasing the risk of disease. Climate change is intensifying these pressures by disrupting hydrological cycles, altering precipitation patterns, and increasing the frequency of floods and droughts. These environmental changes exacerbate existing vulnerabilities, threatening both water supply and public health on a global scale.

Rapid urbanization further compounds the challenges at the water-health nexus. Expanding populations strain water and sanitation infrastructure, particularly in informal settlements where services are often lacking. Untreated wastewater contaminates surface and groundwater sources, while inadequate stormwater management increases the risk of waterborne disease outbreaks during flooding. The convergence of poor infrastructure, pollution, and population density amplifies public health risks, demanding integrated strategies that address both water management and health system resilience.

This book explores the multifaceted relationship between water and health, examining the biological, environmental, and social dimensions that shape this critical connection. It considers how water influences health outcomes through pathways such as quality, access, sanitation, nutrition, climate impacts, and governance. Each chapter provides a structured analysis of these linkages, offering insights into the policies, systems, and practices required to protect and promote health through sustainable water management. By understanding these complex interdependencies, stakeholders can develop more effective interventions that ensure safe water, reduce disease burdens, and enhance the resilience of communities and health systems worldwide.

Chapter 1: The Fundamental Role of Water in Human Health

Water is the foundation of life, essential for maintaining the body's basic physiological processes and supporting broader aspects of human well-being. It regulates body temperature, enables digestion, transports nutrients, and facilitates the removal of waste products. Beyond these biological functions, water contributes to public health through sanitation, hygiene, and food security, reducing the risks of infectious diseases and malnutrition. When access to clean and sufficient water is disrupted, health outcomes deteriorate rapidly. This chapter introduces the vital role of water in sustaining human health, setting the stage for deeper exploration of its diverse functions and impacts.

Physiological Functions of Water

Water is integral to maintaining the fundamental physiological functions that sustain human life. It serves as the primary medium for biochemical reactions, acting as a solvent that enables nutrients, gases, and waste products to dissolve and move throughout the body. Approximately 60 percent of the human body is composed of water, distributed across intracellular, extracellular, and plasma compartments, each of which relies on fluid balance to function effectively. Within cells, water supports enzymatic activity, facilitates the synthesis of macromolecules, and preserves the structural integrity of proteins and membranes. The aqueous environment is essential for maintaining the delicate pH and ionic conditions necessary for cellular metabolism, while also enabling the diffusion of nutrients and signaling molecules across membranes. Without adequate water, these metabolic processes slow, impairing energy production and overall cellular function.

One of water's most critical roles is in thermoregulation, the process by which the body maintains its internal temperature within a narrow range. Water's high heat capacity allows it to absorb and store large amounts of heat, buffering the body against rapid temperature fluctuations. Through sweating and evaporative cooling, water helps dissipate excess heat generated by metabolic processes or environmental conditions, preventing hyperthermia. This thermoregulatory function is vital during physical exertion or exposure to hot environments, where fluid loss through sweat must be replaced to sustain performance and prevent heat-related illnesses. Conversely, dehydration reduces sweat production and blood volume, impairing the body's ability to cool itself and increasing the risk of heat exhaustion or heat stroke.

Water is also central to the transport of nutrients and oxygen to cells and the removal of metabolic waste products. Blood, composed primarily of water, circulates through the vascular system to deliver glucose, amino acids, fatty acids, electrolytes, and other essential substances to tissues. It simultaneously collects carbon dioxide, urea, and other waste products for excretion through the lungs and kidneys. Water facilitates the filtration of blood in the kidneys, enabling the elimination of toxins and maintenance of fluid and electrolyte balance. Adequate hydration ensures optimal blood volume and pressure, which are crucial for cardiovascular stability and organ perfusion. Even mild dehydration can decrease plasma volume, leading to reduced cardiac output, impaired oxygen delivery, and diminished physical and cognitive performance.

Lubrication and cushioning are additional vital functions of water in the human body. Water is a key component of synovial fluid, which lubricates joints, reduces friction, and protects cartilage from wear during movement. It also contributes to the production of mucus and saliva, which aid in swallowing, digestion, and respiratory defense. In the eyes, tears maintain moisture and remove debris, while in the central nervous system, cerebrospinal fluid cushions the brain and spinal cord, protecting them from mechanical injury. Water's presence in these fluids allows the body to maintain structural integrity, mobility, and protection against physical trauma or irritation, which are all essential to maintaining overall health.

Fluid balance, regulated by complex hormonal systems, is another fundamental aspect of water's physiological role. The hypothalamus monitors plasma osmolality and triggers thirst when water levels fall, prompting fluid intake. Hormones such as antidiuretic hormone (ADH) and aldosterone adjust renal water and sodium reabsorption to conserve or excrete fluid as needed. This regulation preserves homeostasis by ensuring that water intake and output remain balanced, preventing both dehydration and overhydration. Disruptions in fluid balance can lead to serious conditions such as hyponatremia or hypernatremia, which affect neural function, muscle activity, and cardiovascular stability.

Water also plays a role in digestion and nutrient absorption. It forms a major component of digestive secretions, including saliva, gastric juice, bile, and pancreatic enzymes, which break down food and facilitate nutrient uptake in the intestines. Water in the gastrointestinal tract helps dissolve nutrients, promotes their transport across intestinal walls, and softens stool to enable regular bowel movements. Insufficient water intake can lead to constipation and reduced efficiency in nutrient absorption, affecting energy levels, immunity, and growth. A hydrated gastrointestinal system supports the continuous renewal of intestinal lining cells, which form a barrier against pathogens and toxins, highlighting water's role in maintaining gut integrity and immune defense.

Water's role in cellular homeostasis and tissue health is equally critical. It maintains the turgor of cells, preventing shrinkage or swelling that could compromise their structure and function. The osmotic balance maintained by water enables the proper distribution of electrolytes such as sodium, potassium, and chloride, which are essential for nerve impulse transmission, muscle contraction, and acid-base balance. Water's movement across cell membranes regulates cell volume and nutrient exchange, ensuring the continuous operation of physiological processes. This delicate balance must be preserved for tissues to function optimally, as even small fluid deficits can disrupt electrolyte gradients and cellular signaling.

Collectively, these physiological functions highlight water's irreplaceable role in sustaining life and health. It is more than just a medium for hydration—it is a vital participant in every system of the human body, from temperature regulation and waste removal to joint lubrication and cellular metabolism. Adequate water intake is therefore essential to preserve homeostasis, support physical and cognitive performance, and protect the body from environmental stressors and disease.

Hydration and Human Performance

Hydration plays a pivotal role in maintaining and enhancing human performance, influencing physical endurance, cognitive function, and overall well-being. Water is the primary component of blood and bodily tissues, and even mild dehydration can disrupt physiological balance, impairing the body's ability to function efficiently. During physical activity or exposure to heat, fluid losses through sweat increase significantly, making it essential to maintain adequate hydration to preserve cardiovascular stability, thermoregulation, and muscular performance. The human body has limited water reserves and depends on continuous intake to offset losses, highlighting the importance of proactive hydration strategies in daily life and during periods of increased exertion.

One of the most immediate effects of dehydration is a reduction in blood plasma volume, which diminishes cardiac output and increases cardiovascular strain. As plasma volume decreases, the heart must work harder to pump blood, raising heart rate and lowering stroke volume. This compromises the delivery of oxygen and nutrients to working muscles, accelerating fatigue and reducing endurance. Dehydration of as little as two percent of body mass has been shown to impair aerobic performance, especially during prolonged exercise or in hot environments. The resulting decline in sweat rate further limits heat dissipation, elevating core body temperature and compounding the risk of heat-related illnesses such as heat exhaustion and heat stroke. Maintaining fluid balance is thus essential to sustaining physical performance and preventing dangerous physiological stress.

Hydration also affects muscle function and energy metabolism. Water supports the transport of glucose, fatty acids, and amino acids to muscle cells, where they are metabolized for energy production. Dehydration reduces muscle blood flow and oxygen delivery, impairing mitochondrial energy production and increasing reliance on anaerobic metabolism, which leads to earlier onset of fatigue and accumulation of metabolic byproducts such as lactate. Adequate hydration preserves electrolyte balance, which is critical for muscle contraction and nerve signal transmission. Electrolyte imbalances caused by fluid loss, particularly sodium depletion, can lead to muscle cramps, weakness, and decreased coordination. These effects underscore the need for both water and electrolyte replenishment during prolonged or intense physical activity to sustain optimal muscular performance.

Cognitive performance is also closely tied to hydration status. Water is essential for maintaining brain volume, cerebral blood flow, and the balance of neurotransmitters involved in mood, attention, and memory. Even mild dehydration can impair cognitive functions such as short-term memory, concentration, alertness, and reaction time. This is particularly evident during tasks requiring sustained attention or complex decision-making, where mental fatigue sets in more quickly in a dehydrated state. Dehydration can also affect mood, contributing to feelings of irritability, anxiety, and reduced motivation, all of which can indirectly impair performance. Maintaining hydration supports mental clarity, decision-making, and emotional stability, which are essential for both everyday functioning and high-pressure tasks.

Thermoregulation is another crucial aspect of human performance influenced by hydration. During physical exertion, the body relies on sweating and evaporative cooling to dissipate excess heat. Adequate hydration supports sweat production and skin blood flow, preventing dangerous rises in core temperature. Dehydration reduces sweating capacity, leading to increased thermal strain, earlier onset of fatigue, and higher perceived exertion. This effect is especially pronounced in hot or humid environments, where sweat losses are elevated and the risk of heat stress is heightened. Proper fluid intake before, during, and after exercise or heat exposure helps maintain thermal balance, supporting sustained physical output and reducing the risk of heat-related disorders.

Recovery from physical exertion also depends on hydration. Water facilitates the clearance of metabolic waste products such as urea and creatinine through the kidneys, preventing their accumulation in the bloodstream. It supports the delivery of nutrients needed for tissue repair and replenishes lost electrolytes to restore homeostasis. Post-exercise rehydration accelerates recovery, reducing muscle soreness and enabling quicker return to peak performance levels. Neglecting fluid replacement can prolong fatigue, compromise immune function, and delay adaptation to training.

Overall, maintaining optimal hydration is essential for supporting both physical and cognitive aspects of human performance. Water enables the body to transport nutrients, regulate temperature, sustain cardiovascular and muscular function, and preserve mental acuity. Regular fluid intake tailored to individual needs and environmental conditions is crucial for maximizing endurance, strength, alertness, and recovery, ensuring that the body and mind can operate at their full potential.

Water Requirements Across the Life Course

Water requirements vary throughout the human life course, reflecting differences in physiological needs, body composition, and environmental exposures at different ages. Infants, children, adolescents, adults, and older adults each have distinct hydration demands shaped by growth, activity levels, metabolic rates, and health status. Understanding these variations is essential to support health and development across all stages of life. While general guidelines exist, individual water needs can fluctuate depending on factors such as diet, climate, and physical activity, making it important to adapt fluid intake to personal circumstances.

In infancy, water is vital for supporting rapid growth and high metabolic activity. Newborns have a higher proportion of body water, approximately 70 to 75 percent of body weight, and their kidneys are still developing the ability to concentrate urine. This makes them more vulnerable to fluid loss from illness, fever, or hot environments. Breast milk or infant formula generally meets infants' water needs during the first six months of life, providing adequate hydration while delivering essential nutrients. Direct water supplementation is typically unnecessary and can even be harmful in very young infants if it displaces nutrient intake or leads to electrolyte imbalances. As complementary foods are introduced around six months, additional water becomes more important to support digestion and compensate for losses from increased physical activity and exposure to environmental heat.

During childhood, water supports continued growth, development, and learning. Children's higher metabolic rates and physical activity levels increase their water turnover compared with adults. Their bodies generate more heat relative to size, making them more prone to heat stress and dehydration, especially during play or exercise in warm environments. Ensuring children drink water regularly is crucial, as they may not recognize or communicate thirst effectively. Adequate hydration promotes cognitive function, concentration, and mood regulation, which are important for school performance. Water should be offered frequently throughout the day, not only during meals, to maintain optimal hydration and prevent declines in attention or physical endurance.

Adolescence brings rapid physical growth, hormonal changes, and often increased participation in sports, all of which elevate water requirements. The body composition of adolescents shifts as muscle mass increases, and their sweat rates often rise with puberty, especially in boys. These changes heighten their risk of fluid and electrolyte losses during physical exertion. Peer habits and access to sugary beverages can also influence adolescents' hydration choices, sometimes displacing water consumption. Encouraging regular water intake and awareness of thirst signals during this life stage is important to support healthy physical performance, growth, and long-term hydration habits.

In adulthood, water requirements stabilize but remain substantial to sustain normal physiological functions. The average adult requires several liters of total water per day from beverages and food to balance losses through urine, sweat, breath, and feces. Needs increase with higher physical activity levels, hot or humid environments, and during pregnancy or lactation. Pregnant individuals require additional water to support increased blood volume, amniotic fluid, and fetal growth, while lactating individuals need even more to maintain breast milk production. Adequate hydration in adults supports cardiovascular function, temperature regulation, cognitive performance, and kidney health, helping to prevent conditions such as urinary tract infections and kidney stones.

Older adulthood introduces unique hydration challenges. Aging reduces total body water content and blunts the sensation of thirst, which can delay fluid intake. Kidney function also declines, reducing the ability to concentrate urine and conserve water, while chronic health conditions and certain medications may increase fluid loss or restrict fluid intake. These factors make older adults particularly vulnerable to dehydration, which can rapidly lead to confusion, falls, and hospitalization. Providing frequent opportunities to drink, choosing palatable fluids, and monitoring hydration status are essential measures to maintain health and functional independence in later life.

Throughout the life course, water requirements evolve alongside changes in physiology, behavior, and environment. Meeting these needs consistently is critical to support growth, performance, and resilience at every age. Adapting hydration practices to individual life stages helps safeguard health, prevent illness, and promote well-being across the lifespan.

Impacts of Water Deficiency on Health

Water deficiency, or dehydration, occurs when fluid losses exceed fluid intake, disrupting the body's ability to maintain homeostasis. This imbalance affects nearly every organ system, with consequences ranging from mild discomfort to life-threatening conditions. The severity of these impacts depends on the degree and duration of dehydration, as well as individual factors such as age, health status, and environmental conditions. Even mild water deficits can impair physical and cognitive performance, while severe deficits can compromise vital functions and increase the risk of morbidity and mortality.

One of the earliest and most noticeable effects of water deficiency is reduced cardiovascular function. As water levels decline, blood plasma volume decreases, leading to lower blood pressure and reduced cardiac output. The heart compensates by increasing heart rate, but this cannot fully offset the decline in oxygen and nutrient delivery to tissues. As a result, fatigue and weakness set in more quickly, and physical endurance diminishes. Reduced blood volume also impairs the body's ability to regulate temperature. With less blood available to carry heat to the skin for dissipation, core body temperature rises, increasing the risk of heat exhaustion or heat stroke, especially during exercise or exposure to high ambient temperatures.

Water deficiency also disrupts electrolyte balance, which is essential for nerve signaling, muscle contraction, and cellular function. As fluid losses continue through sweat, urine, or diarrhea, sodium and other electrolytes become concentrated in the blood, leading to hypernatremia. This imbalance causes neurological symptoms such as irritability, confusion, dizziness, and, in severe cases, seizures or coma. Muscle cramps, spasms, and weakness can also result from altered electrolyte gradients, impairing coordination and mobility. These neuromuscular effects can appear even with mild dehydration and significantly impair performance and safety during physical tasks.

Cognitive functions are particularly sensitive to hydration status. Dehydration as low as one to two percent of body mass can impair attention, short-term memory, reaction time, and mood. Reduced cerebral blood flow and changes in neurotransmitter activity contribute to mental fatigue, difficulty concentrating, and decreased alertness. These effects are especially concerning in children, who may struggle to recognize or communicate thirst, and in older adults, who may experience exacerbated cognitive decline when dehydrated. Chronic low-level dehydration can also affect mental health over time, contributing to irritability, anxiety, and decreased motivation.

Gastrointestinal and renal systems are heavily impacted by insufficient water intake. Water is necessary for digestion, nutrient absorption, and the movement of food through the intestines. Deficiency can lead to constipation and increased risk of gastrointestinal discomfort or impaction. In the kidneys, water is vital for filtering blood and excreting metabolic waste. When water intake is inadequate, urine becomes concentrated, raising the risk of kidney stones and urinary tract infections. Prolonged or recurrent dehydration can contribute to chronic kidney disease by increasing renal workload and promoting tissue damage.

Water deficiency compromises the immune system as well. Mucous membranes in the respiratory and gastrointestinal tracts rely on hydration to maintain barrier integrity and flush out pathogens. Dry membranes are more susceptible to infection, prolonging illness and recovery.

These impacts highlight that water is not only a basic necessity but also a protective factor for multiple physiological systems. Maintaining adequate hydration is essential to prevent the cascade of health problems triggered by water deficiency.

Chapter 2: Water Quality and Human Health Risks

The quality of water is one of the most important determinants of public health. Safe water protects against infectious diseases, chemical exposures, and long-term health complications, while contaminated water remains a leading cause of preventable illness and death worldwide. Microbial pathogens such as bacteria, viruses, and parasites continue to cause widespread outbreaks, particularly where sanitation and treatment systems are inadequate. At the same time, chemical pollutants, heavy metals, and emerging contaminants introduce chronic risks that threaten entire populations over time. This chapter examines the relationship between water quality and health, highlighting the risks that arise when safety is compromised.

Microbial Contaminants and Waterborne Diseases

Microbial contaminants in water are among the most significant threats to public health worldwide, causing a wide range of waterborne diseases that contribute to high morbidity and mortality, particularly in regions with inadequate sanitation and water treatment infrastructure. These contaminants include bacteria, viruses, protozoa, and helminths, many of which are transmitted through the fecal-oral route when water becomes contaminated with human or animal waste. The ingestion of contaminated water can result in acute illnesses, chronic health problems, and outbreaks that place immense strain on healthcare systems. Understanding the types of microbial contaminants, their transmission pathways, and the diseases they cause is critical to developing effective water safety and public health strategies.

Bacterial pathogens are major contributors to waterborne diseases. Species such as Vibrio cholerae, Escherichia coli (particularly enterotoxigenic and enterohemorrhagic strains), Salmonella, Shigella, and Campylobacter are commonly associated with contaminated drinking water. These bacteria can cause gastrointestinal illnesses ranging from mild diarrhea to severe, life-threatening dysentery or cholera. Cholera, caused by toxigenic Vibrio cholerae, is characterized by acute watery diarrhea and rapid dehydration that can lead to death within hours if untreated. Shigella and Salmonella infections often produce bloody diarrhea, fever, and abdominal cramps, while pathogenic E. coli can cause hemolytic uremic syndrome, a serious condition leading to kidney failure. These bacterial infections spread rapidly where sanitation systems are inadequate, particularly in densely populated urban areas and refugee camps, and are often exacerbated by flooding and other environmental disruptions that mobilize pathogens into water supplies.

Viruses also pose a major risk through contaminated water. Enteric viruses such as noroviruses, rotaviruses, adenoviruses, and hepatitis A and E viruses are frequently detected in polluted water sources. These viruses are highly infectious and can persist in water for extended periods, resisting conventional chlorination and disinfection in some cases. Rotaviruses are a leading cause of severe diarrhea in young children, resulting in substantial childhood mortality in low-income regions. Noroviruses are a common cause of acute gastroenteritis globally and can trigger large outbreaks in confined settings such as schools, cruise ships, and healthcare facilities. Hepatitis A and E viruses spread through fecally contaminated drinking water, causing liver inflammation, jaundice, fever, and gastrointestinal symptoms, with hepatitis E particularly dangerous for pregnant women. Because viral infections often require only a small infectious dose, their presence in drinking water represents a serious public health hazard.

Protozoan parasites further contribute to the burden of waterborne diseases. Giardia lamblia and Cryptosporidium parvumare among the most common protozoa found in untreated or inadequately treated water. These organisms form hardy cysts or oocysts that resist standard chlorination, allowing them to survive in the environment and infect new hosts. Infection with Giardia causes giardiasis, characterized by chronic diarrhea, abdominal cramps, bloating, and weight loss. Cryptosporidium causes cryptosporidiosis, which leads to profuse watery diarrhea and can be particularly severe in immunocompromised individuals such as people living with HIV/AIDS. Entamoeba histolytica, another waterborne protozoan, causes amoebiasis, leading to dysentery and liver abscesses. These parasitic infections often result in prolonged illness, malnutrition, and impaired growth in children, further compounding the health burden in affected populations.

Helminths, or parasitic worms, can also be transmitted through contaminated water, particularly in tropical and subtropical regions. Dracunculus medinensis (Guinea worm) is a notable example historically linked to drinking water contaminated with copepods carrying infective larvae. Although eradication efforts have dramatically reduced its prevalence, isolated cases still occur in a few regions. Schistosomes, the parasitic worms responsible for schistosomiasis, infect humans who come into contact with freshwater containing larval forms released by infected snails. The larvae penetrate the skin, mature in the body, and cause chronic disease affecting the liver, intestines, urinary tract, and other organs. Schistosomiasis contributes to anemia, stunted growth, and cognitive impairment in children, while causing chronic pain and organ damage in adults. These water-related helminth infections highlight how contact with contaminated water—not just ingestion—can lead to serious disease.

The transmission of these microbial contaminants is facilitated by inadequate water treatment, poor sanitation infrastructure, and unsafe hygiene practices. Human and animal feces can contaminate surface waters, groundwater, and distribution systems when sewage is improperly managed or when open defecation is prevalent. Heavy rainfall and flooding events can mobilize pathogens from soils, latrines, and septic systems into drinking water sources. Once introduced into water systems, microbes can persist in biofilms within pipes and storage tanks, posing ongoing contamination risks even after source water quality improves. Interruptions in water supply or loss of disinfectant residuals can also enable microbial regrowth and contamination within distribution networks.

The health impacts of microbial contamination are not limited to acute infections. Repeated exposure to diarrheal pathogens contributes to chronic undernutrition and impaired immune development in children, a condition known as environmental enteric dysfunction. This condition damages the intestinal lining, reducing nutrient absorption and increasing vulnerability to infections. Waterborne diseases also impose indirect burdens by overwhelming healthcare facilities, reducing school attendance, and limiting economic productivity. These effects are especially pronounced in low-resource settings, where access to medical care, clean water, and sanitation is limited.

Preventing microbial contamination of water requires a multi-barrier approach encompassing source water protection, safe water treatment, secure distribution, and household-level hygiene practices. Effective treatment methods include filtration, coagulation-flocculation, ultraviolet disinfection, and chlorination, with additional measures needed to address resistant protozoa such as Cryptosporidium. Continuous water quality monitoring and maintenance of disinfectant residuals in distribution systems are essential to prevent recontamination. Expanding access to improved sanitation, eliminating open defecation, and promoting handwashing with soap further reduce the spread of pathogens into water supplies. These strategies, combined with health education and surveillance systems, are critical to controlling microbial contaminants and safeguarding public health.

Microbial contaminants in water remain a leading cause of preventable disease globally. Their diversity, persistence, and ability to spread rapidly make them a persistent threat, particularly in environments lacking robust infrastructure and effective governance. Addressing this challenge requires sustained investment in water quality management, sanitation, and hygiene systems to ensure that safe water is accessible to all communities and that the burden of waterborne diseases is significantly reduced.

Chemical Contaminants and Toxicological Effects

Chemical contaminants in water pose serious risks to human health, often with effects that are less immediate than microbial pathogens but potentially more insidious and long-term. These contaminants enter water sources through natural processes, industrial activities, agricultural runoff, and improper waste disposal, accumulating in surface water, groundwater, and distribution systems. Exposure to chemical pollutants can result in a broad spectrum of toxicological effects, from acute poisoning to chronic diseases such as cancer, neurological disorders, reproductive problems, and developmental abnormalities. Understanding the types of chemical contaminants, their sources, and their impacts on human health is crucial to ensuring water safety and protecting public health.

Heavy metals are among the most well-documented chemical contaminants in drinking water. Elements such as arsenic, lead, mercury, cadmium, and chromium can enter water supplies through natural leaching from soils and rocks or from industrial discharges, mining operations, and waste sites. Arsenic contamination of groundwater, for example, is a major public health concern in several parts of the world, including South Asia. Chronic exposure to arsenic is associated with skin lesions, cardiovascular disease, diabetes, and various cancers, particularly of the skin, bladder, and lungs. Lead exposure, often from corroding pipes or plumbing fixtures, can impair neurological development in children, leading to cognitive deficits, behavioral problems, and reduced IQ. Even low-level lead exposure has been linked to hypertension and kidney damage in adults. Mercury and cadmium can accumulate in tissues, disrupting kidney and liver function, damaging the nervous system, and interfering with fetal development during pregnancy. These heavy metals are persistent, bioaccumulative, and toxic even at low concentrations, making their presence in water especially hazardous.

Nitrate and nitrite contamination represents another significant chemical risk, primarily originating from agricultural fertilizers, animal waste, and leaking septic systems. When ingested, nitrates can be converted into nitrites in the body, which interfere with the oxygen-carrying capacity of hemoglobin. This can cause methemoglobinemia, or "blue baby syndrome," in infants, a condition that reduces oxygen delivery to tissues and can be fatal if untreated. Long-term exposure to high nitrate levels has also been associated with certain cancers, thyroid disorders, and adverse reproductive outcomes. Nitrate pollution is widespread in agricultural regions and often affects groundwater used for drinking, highlighting the need for strict controls on fertilizer application and proper wastewater management to prevent contamination.

Industrial and synthetic organic chemicals are also common water pollutants. These include solvents, pesticides, herbicides, polychlorinated biphenyls (PCBs), per- and polyfluoroalkyl substances (PFAS), and disinfection byproducts such as trihalomethanes (THMs). Many of these compounds are resistant to degradation and can persist in the environment for decades, accumulating in water sources and entering the food chain. Pesticides and herbicides used in agriculture can run off into water bodies, affecting aquatic ecosystems and posing risks to human health through drinking water exposure. Chronic exposure has been linked to endocrine disruption, reproductive toxicity, neurodevelopmental disorders, and various cancers. PCBs, once widely used in electrical equipment, are now banned in many countries but remain in sediments and can leach into water. They are known carcinogens and endocrine disruptors, capable of impairing immune and reproductive systems. PFAS, often referred to as "forever chemicals," are used in firefighting foams, non-stick cookware, and water-resistant products. They accumulate in water and the human body, contributing to immune suppression, liver damage, developmental effects, and certain cancers. Disinfection byproducts form when chlorine or other disinfectants react with organic matter in water, and chronic exposure to these compounds has been linked to bladder cancer and reproductive issues.

Another group of contaminants of concern includes pharmaceuticals and personal care products, which enter water systems through wastewater discharges, improper disposal, and agricultural runoff from medicated livestock. These compounds, present in trace amounts, can exert subtle but significant biological effects over time. Hormones and endocrine-disrupting chemicals can interfere with reproductive systems, potentially reducing fertility and altering developmental processes. Antibiotic residues in water contribute to antimicrobial resistance, a growing global health threat that undermines the effectiveness of essential medicines. Although concentrations are usually low, the continual presence of these substances in water raises concerns about long-term cumulative exposure and its implications for public health.

The toxicological effects of chemical contaminants depend on several factors, including the type of substance, concentration, duration of exposure, and individual susceptibility. Children, pregnant individuals, and people with compromised immune systems are particularly vulnerable to harm. Unlike microbial contamination, which typically causes acute illness with rapid onset, the effects of chemical exposure often develop slowly, making them more difficult to detect and link directly to water sources. This latency increases the importance of proactive monitoring, regulation, and risk assessment to prevent harmful exposures before they occur.

Protecting water supplies from chemical contamination requires comprehensive management strategies. These include enforcing stringent water quality standards, monitoring industrial discharges and agricultural runoff, upgrading water treatment technologies, and replacing aging infrastructure such as lead pipes. Advanced treatment methods like activated carbon filtration, reverse osmosis, and advanced oxidation processes can remove many chemical pollutants from drinking water. Source protection is equally critical, involving the control of pollution at its origin through sustainable agricultural practices, proper hazardous waste disposal, and containment of industrial byproducts. Public education on safe chemical use and disposal also reduces the risk of contamination.

Chemical contaminants represent a pervasive and often invisible threat to water safety. Their long-term health impacts and persistence in the environment demand vigilant monitoring, robust regulation, and sustained investment in water quality protection to safeguard public health.

Emerging Contaminants and Pharmaceuticals

Emerging contaminants are a diverse group of chemicals increasingly detected in water sources, many of which were not previously monitored or regulated. Among the most concerning of these are pharmaceuticals and personal care products (PPCPs), along with other substances such as endocrine-disrupting compounds, microplastics, and industrial additives. These contaminants enter water systems through human excretion, improper disposal of medicines, agricultural runoff from medicated livestock, and discharges from wastewater treatment plants. Because most conventional water treatment facilities were not designed to remove these compounds, they persist in surface waters, groundwater, and even treated drinking water at trace concentrations. While typically present at low levels, their continuous release and potential for long-term exposure raise growing concerns about their effects on human health and the environment.

Pharmaceutical residues in water include a wide range of therapeutic agents, such as antibiotics, analgesics, antidepressants, hormones, and antiepileptic drugs. These compounds are biologically active by design, and even low concentrations can exert subtle effects on human physiology over time. Antibiotics are of particular concern because their presence in water can contribute to the development and spread of antimicrobial resistance. Resistant bacteria can emerge in aquatic environments and potentially transfer resistance genes to human pathogens, undermining the effectiveness of essential medicines. Hormones, including natural and synthetic estrogens from contraceptive pills, are potent endocrine disruptors that can affect reproductive systems and development. While much of the evidence of endocrine disruption comes from aquatic wildlife, the potential for chronic low-dose exposure to influence human hormonal balance, fertility, or development warrants careful scrutiny.

Personal care products, such as synthetic musks, preservatives, and ultraviolet filters from sunscreens, also contribute to emerging contaminant loads. These substances can persist in the environment and bioaccumulate in tissues, raising concerns about their long-term effects on human health. Some have been linked to endocrine disruption, reproductive toxicity, and allergic reactions. Although concentrations found in drinking water are generally low, the cumulative impact of exposure to complex mixtures of PPCPs and other emerging contaminants over a lifetime remains poorly understood, and potential additive or synergistic effects are a key area of ongoing research.

Other emerging contaminants include industrial chemicals such as per- and PFAS, flame retardants, and plasticizers. PFAS, often called "forever chemicals" because of their persistence, have been detected globally in water supplies and human blood. They are associated with liver toxicity, immune suppression, developmental effects, and certain cancers. Microplastics, tiny plastic particles shed from consumer products and degraded plastic waste, are now found in drinking water, bottled water, and even atmospheric deposition. While their health impacts on humans are still being studied, concerns include physical blockage, chemical leaching of plastic additives, and the potential to carry microbial pathogens or toxic substances.

The main challenge with emerging contaminants is that they are largely unregulated and often escape removal in conventional water treatment processes. Most treatment plants are designed to remove pathogens and basic chemical pollutants, not trace organic compounds. As a result, these substances can persist through treatment and enter drinking water systems. Advanced treatment methods such as activated carbon adsorption, advanced oxidation, membrane filtration, and ozonation show promise in removing many of these compounds, but implementing such technologies widely requires significant investment.

Addressing emerging contaminants requires proactive monitoring, improved wastewater treatment, and updated regulatory frameworks. Expanding surveillance programs to include pharmaceuticals and other novel chemicals can help assess their prevalence and risks. Source control measures, such as take-back programs for unused medications and stricter controls on industrial discharges, can reduce inputs into water systems. Public education on proper disposal of pharmaceuticals and reduced use of harmful chemicals can also play an important role. Because these contaminants represent evolving and complex risks, collaborative efforts between scientists, regulators, water utilities, and the public are essential to safeguard water quality and protect human health from their potential long-term impacts.

Standards and Guidelines for Drinking Water Quality

Standards and guidelines for drinking water quality are essential tools for safeguarding public health by ensuring that water intended for human consumption is safe, clean, and free from harmful levels of contaminants. These benchmarks are developed by international organizations, national regulatory agencies, and public health authorities based on scientific evidence about the health risks posed by various biological, chemical, and physical contaminants. They establish maximum allowable concentrations of substances in drinking water and outline the monitoring, treatment, and management practices necessary to meet these safety targets. Adherence to these standards reduces the risk of waterborne disease outbreaks, chronic health effects, and public exposure to hazardous substances.

At the global level, the World Health Organization (WHO) provides the most widely recognized framework through its Guidelines for Drinking-Water Quality. These guidelines offer health-based targets and recommended maximum concentrations for a broad range of microbial and chemical contaminants, including bacteria, viruses, protozoa, heavy metals, pesticides, and emerging pollutants. The WHO guidelines emphasize a risk-based approach to water safety, encouraging countries to implement Water Safety Plans that encompass all stages of water supply, from source protection to distribution and household use. The guidelines are periodically updated to incorporate new scientific findings, toxicological data, and advances in treatment technologies, ensuring that they remain relevant to evolving public health challenges.

Many countries adapt the WHO framework into legally binding national drinking water standards. In the United States, the Environmental Protection Agency (EPA) enforces the National Primary Drinking Water Regulations under the Safe Drinking Water Act. These regulations set enforceable Maximum Contaminant Levels (MCLs) for over 90 biological and chemical contaminants, including pathogenic microorganisms, disinfection byproducts, inorganic chemicals, organic pollutants, and radionuclides. They also establish treatment technique requirements and monitoring protocols to ensure compliance. The EPA periodically reviews and revises these standards to reflect new scientific evidence and emerging risks, such as per- and PFAS.

Similarly, the European Union (EU) maintains stringent drinking water standards through the EU Drinking Water Directive, which mandates maximum permissible levels of contaminants and requires member states to monitor, report, and take corrective action when standards are exceeded. The directive emphasizes the precautionary principle, aiming to minimize exposure to contaminants as much as reasonably achievable. Other regions, such as Australia, Canada, and Japan, have their own national guidelines that reflect local conditions, including variations in geology, industrial activity, and climate that influence water quality risks.

Drinking water standards also address aesthetic and operational parameters such as taste, odor, color, turbidity, and pH, which, while not directly harmful, affect consumer confidence and can signal underlying problems in water treatment or distribution systems. Operational targets help utilities maintain system performance, prevent corrosion, and inhibit microbial regrowth. Comprehensive monitoring and reporting systems are integral to these standards, ensuring that water suppliers regularly test for contaminants and maintain transparency with regulators and the public.

While standards provide essential protection, their effectiveness depends on consistent implementation, enforcement, and investment in infrastructure and monitoring capacity. Many low- and middle-income countries face challenges in meeting established standards due to limited resources, aging infrastructure, and gaps in regulatory oversight. Strengthening laboratory capacity, training personnel, and improving water treatment and distribution systems are critical steps for achieving compliance and protecting public health. International collaboration and technical support can help bridge these gaps.

Standards and guidelines for drinking water quality serve as the foundation of safe water supply systems. They translate scientific knowledge into actionable safety limits and operational practices, guiding governments, utilities, and communities in delivering safe drinking water. Their continual refinement and enforcement are vital to preventing contamination, reducing health risks, and ensuring public trust in water services.

Chapter 3: Sanitation, Hygiene, and Disease Prevention

Sanitation and hygiene are critical components of the water-health relationship, directly influencing the prevention of disease and the promotion of well-being. Access to safe sanitation facilities and the practice of good hygiene, supported by adequate water supply, significantly reduce the spread of infectious diseases. Where sanitation and hygiene systems are inadequate, pathogens are easily transmitted, creating cycles of illness that particularly affect children and vulnerable groups. This chapter explores how sanitation and hygiene interact with water to safeguard health, emphasizing their role in breaking transmission pathways, improving quality of life, and strengthening public health resilience.

Water, Sanitation, and Hygiene (WASH) and Public Health

WASH are fundamental pillars of public health, forming the foundation upon which disease prevention, health promotion, and human development rest. Access to safe drinking water, adequate sanitation facilities, and good hygiene practices reduces the transmission of infectious diseases, improves nutritional outcomes, and enhances the overall well-being and productivity of individuals and communities. Despite their essential role, inadequate WASH conditions remain widespread, particularly in low- and middle-income regions, contributing to preventable illness, death, and entrenched cycles of poverty. Understanding the interconnectedness of WASH and public health is critical to designing policies and interventions that protect populations and promote sustainable development.

Safe water supply is central to protecting health because it interrupts the transmission of numerous waterborne pathogens. Contaminated drinking water can carry bacteria, viruses, protozoa, and helminths responsible for diseases such as cholera, typhoid, dysentery, hepatitis

A and E, giardiasis, and cryptosporidiosis. These infections cause diarrheal disease, which is a leading cause of child mortality worldwide and a major contributor to malnutrition and stunted growth. Providing a reliable source of safe water reduces exposure to these pathogens, lowering the incidence of gastrointestinal illnesses and their associated complications. Beyond microbial safety, water must also be available in sufficient quantities to meet domestic needs such as cooking, cleaning, and personal hygiene, as water scarcity can force reliance on unsafe sources or limit hygiene practices, increasing the risk of disease transmission.

Sanitation complements water supply by preventing the introduction of human excreta and other wastes into the environment where they can contaminate water sources and spread pathogens. Inadequate sanitation contributes to the spread of fecal-oral diseases by allowing fecal matter to reach drinking water, food, soil, and surfaces that come into contact with humans. Open defecation and poorly managed sanitation systems enable the contamination of groundwater and surface water with enteric pathogens. Improved sanitation facilities—such as flush toilets, ventilated improved pit latrines, and safely managed sewer systems—create a physical barrier between human excreta and people, breaking key transmission pathways. Proper containment, transport, treatment, and safe reuse or disposal of wastewater and fecal sludge are essential steps in reducing environmental contamination and safeguarding public health. Investments in sanitation infrastructure significantly decrease the incidence of diarrheal diseases, parasitic infections, and neglected tropical diseases, reducing the burden on healthcare systems and improving community health.

Hygiene practices are the behavioral component of WASH that directly interrupt the spread of infectious agents between individuals. Hand hygiene is particularly critical, as hands are a major vehicle for transferring pathogens from contaminated surfaces, objects, or feces to the mouth, eyes, or nose. Washing hands with soap at key times— after defecation, after cleaning a child, before preparing food, and before eating—can reduce diarrheal disease incidence by up to half and significantly lower respiratory infection rates. Hygiene also includes practices such as safe food handling, menstrual hygiene management, and maintaining cleanliness in household and community environments. These behaviors enhance the effectiveness of water and sanitation infrastructure by reducing opportunities for contamination and infection. However, sustained behavior change often requires more than infrastructure alone; it demands targeted health education, social marketing, and culturally appropriate messaging to build habits and shift norms.

The public health impacts of inadequate WASH extend beyond infectious diseases. Repeated bouts of diarrhea and intestinal infections contribute to environmental enteric dysfunction, a subclinical condition that damages the intestinal lining and impairs nutrient absorption. This leads to chronic undernutrition, stunting, and weakened immune responses, especially in children. Poor WASH conditions also increase the risk of soil-transmitted helminth infections and schistosomiasis, which cause anemia, fatigue, and reduced cognitive and physical development. Inadequate menstrual hygiene facilities can keep girls out of school during menstruation, limiting educational attainment and reinforcing gender inequalities. In healthcare settings, the lack of safe water and sanitation contributes to healthcare-associated infections and undermines infection prevention and control measures, putting patients and health workers at risk and reducing trust in health systems.

The burden of inadequate WASH disproportionately affects vulnerable populations, including children, women, people living in poverty, and those in fragile or conflict-affected settings. Children under five are most susceptible to WASH-related diseases and their long-term consequences, while women and girls bear the physical and social burdens of collecting water and managing household hygiene in many communities. Lack of safe and private sanitation exposes women to harassment, violence, and loss of dignity, and complicates menstrual hygiene management. Marginalized populations often reside in informal settlements or remote rural areas with poor infrastructure, facing persistent barriers to accessing safe water and sanitation services. These inequities exacerbate health

31

disparities and perpetuate intergenerational cycles of poverty and disease.

Addressing WASH challenges requires an integrated, multisectoral approach. Expanding infrastructure alone is insufficient without ensuring continuous service delivery, behavior change, and institutional support. Governments must develop and enforce policies, regulations, and financing mechanisms that support the construction, operation, and maintenance of safe water and sanitation systems. This includes investing in human capacity, strengthening supply chains, and promoting innovation in service delivery models. Public health programs should integrate WASH interventions into broader strategies for maternal and child health, nutrition, education, and infectious disease control. Community engagement is essential to foster ownership, sustainability, and culturally appropriate solutions. Monitoring and evaluation systems must track both service coverage and quality to ensure equitable access and long-term effectiveness.

Global frameworks underscore the importance of WASH in achieving health and development goals. WHO and United Nations Children's Fund (UNICEF) lead the Joint Monitoring Programme for Water Supply, Sanitation and Hygiene, which tracks global progress toward the Sustainable Development Goal 6 target of universal access to safely managed water and sanitation by 2030. Achieving this goal would prevent millions of deaths, improve child growth and learning, and boost economic productivity. The recognition of water and sanitation as human rights by the United Nations reinforces the obligation of governments to ensure equitable access and affordability, particularly for marginalized groups.

WASH interventions are among the most cost-effective public health measures available. They reduce healthcare costs, prevent disease outbreaks, and generate economic benefits through improved productivity, educational attainment, and gender equity. However, progress remains uneven, and climate change, urbanization, and population growth are adding new pressures to water and sanitation systems. Sustained investment, innovation, and political commitment are needed to close coverage gaps and adapt systems to changing conditions. Strengthening WASH systems will be central to advancing public health, reducing inequalities, and achieving sustainable development for all populations.

Fecal-Oral Transmission Pathways

Fecal-oral transmission pathways describe the routes through which pathogens from human or animal feces enter the human body via the mouth, causing infection. This mode of transmission is responsible for a substantial burden of disease worldwide, particularly diarrheal and enteric infections. It occurs when fecal matter containing pathogenic microorganisms contaminates water, food, hands, soil, or surfaces, which are then ingested. The pathways are especially prevalent in environments with inadequate sanitation, unsafe water supplies, and poor hygiene practices, making their interruption central to public health and disease prevention efforts.

The classical conceptual framework for understanding these pathways is the "F-diagram," which identifies the key transmission routes as fluids, fields (soil), flies, fingers, and food. Feces from infected individuals can contaminate water sources (fluids) through open defecation, leaking latrines, or improper sewage disposal. Drinking or using this contaminated water for cooking, washing, or bathing can directly introduce pathogens into the body. Fields become contaminated when untreated human or animal waste is used as fertilizer or when wastewater irrigation introduces pathogens into soil. This contamination can then spread to crops that are eaten raw or undercooked. Flies serve as mechanical vectors by landing on feces and then on food or utensils, transferring pathogens on their legs or mouthparts. Fingers transmit pathogens when people handle feces, contaminated surfaces, or soil and then touch their mouth or prepare food without washing their hands. Food can be contaminated at multiple points—during production, processing, or handling—if hygiene is inadequate or if contaminated water is used in preparation.

Water plays a central role in fecal-oral transmission, serving as both a medium and an amplifier of pathogens. In areas lacking safe drinking water infrastructure, fecal contamination of surface water, groundwater, or stored household water is common. Pathogens such as Vibrio cholerae, Shigella, Salmonella, Escherichia coli, noroviruses, and rotaviruses can survive and even multiply in water under certain conditions. Flooding and heavy rainfall events can mobilize fecal matter from latrines, sewers, and open defecation sites into water sources, causing outbreaks. Conversely, water scarcity can force people to use unsafe sources or ration water for hygiene, increasing opportunities for infection. Safe water supply systems with effective treatment and secure distribution are thus critical barriers against fecal-oral disease transmission.

Environmental contamination sustains these pathways by allowing pathogens to persist outside the human host. Many enteric pathogens are resilient, surviving for days or weeks on surfaces, in soil, or in moist environments. Inadequate sanitation accelerates this cycle by enabling the widespread dispersal of feces in the environment. Children are particularly exposed because they frequently play on the ground and put objects or their hands in their mouths, increasing the risk of ingesting infectious material. This repeated exposure can cause chronic enteric infections that impair nutrient absorption and growth, even without overt diarrhea, contributing to environmental enteric dysfunction.

Interrupting fecal-oral transmission requires breaking each link in these pathways. Improved sanitation systems prevent feces from contaminating the environment and water supplies. Access to safely managed drinking water ensures that ingested fluids are pathogen-free. Handwashing with soap, especially after defecation and before preparing food, blocks the transfer of pathogens via fingers. Proper food hygiene, including washing produce, cooking food thoroughly, and protecting it from flies, reduces contamination risks. Safe disposal of child feces and management of animal waste are also essential, as both are common sources of pathogens. Integrated WASH interventions that combine sanitation infrastructure, water treatment, and hygiene promotion have the greatest impact because they block multiple transmission routes simultaneously.

Fecal-oral transmission pathways highlight the interdependence of water, sanitation, and hygiene systems in protecting public health. As long as fecal contamination persists in the environment, pathogens can circulate through multiple routes, continually reinfecting populations. Controlling these pathways through comprehensive and sustained interventions is essential to reduce enteric disease burdens and improve health outcomes, especially for children and other vulnerable groups.

Hygiene Practices and Behavioral Determinants

Hygiene practices are critical behaviors that prevent the spread of infectious diseases by reducing human exposure to pathogens present in water, food, soil, and on surfaces. They form an essential component of the WASH framework, complementing safe water supply and adequate sanitation to interrupt the fecal-oral transmission of disease-causing microorganisms. Effective hygiene practices encompass hand hygiene, food hygiene, personal cleanliness, menstrual hygiene management, and household environmental cleanliness. The consistent adoption of these behaviors significantly lowers the risk of diarrheal and respiratory infections, intestinal parasitic diseases, and skin and eye infections, improving public health and well-being. However, hygiene practices are influenced by a range of behavioral determinants, including cultural norms, education, social influences, infrastructure availability, and perceived health benefits, which shape whether and how individuals adopt and sustain hygienic behaviors.

Hand hygiene is the most widely recognized and impactful hygiene practice. Washing hands with soap at critical times—after defecation, after cleaning a child, before preparing food, and before eating—can reduce diarrheal disease incidence by up to half and decrease respiratory infections substantially. Soap and running water remove pathogens mechanically, while the chemical action of soap disrupts microbial membranes. Despite its effectiveness, consistent handwashing is often low, especially in low-resource settings. Barriers include lack of access to soap and water at handwashing points, time constraints, ingrained habits, and low risk perception. Behavior change interventions that use visual reminders, social norm messaging, and structured routines can improve compliance. Placing handwashing stations in convenient locations, such as near toilets and kitchens, and ensuring they are well-maintained also increase regular use.

Food hygiene is another key practice that reduces the ingestion of pathogens. This includes washing hands before handling food, thoroughly washing fruits and vegetables, cooking food to safe temperatures, storing food at appropriate temperatures to prevent bacterial growth, and protecting food from flies and other contaminants. In many low-income settings, foodborne diseases are common because of inadequate food safety infrastructure, limited refrigeration, and reliance on informal food markets where contamination risks are high. Education about safe food handling practices, combined with improvements in market hygiene and household storage facilities, helps mitigate these risks. Clean utensils, surfaces, and water used during food preparation are equally important to prevent cross-contamination.

Personal hygiene extends beyond hands to practices such as bathing, oral hygiene, and wearing clean clothing, which prevent skin infections, eye infections, and other communicable conditions. Menstrual hygiene management is especially important for women and girls, requiring access to clean water, soap, private facilities, and safe materials for absorbing or collecting menstrual blood. Poor menstrual hygiene can increase the risk of urogenital infections and contribute to school absenteeism, stigma, and reduced participation in social and economic activities. Providing appropriate facilities, menstrual products, and supportive education helps normalize menstruation and support gender equity.

Household hygiene practices, including safe disposal of human and animal feces, regular cleaning of toilets, safe water storage, and maintaining clean living spaces, reduce environmental contamination with pathogens. Covering drinking water containers, using narrow-necked vessels, and disinfecting water storage equipment prevent recontamination of treated water. Cleaning frequently touched household surfaces, especially in areas with children or sick individuals, further lowers infection risk. These behaviors are especially important in dense urban or informal settlements where environmental contamination is widespread and the potential for disease transmission is high.

Behavioral determinants strongly influence hygiene practices. Knowledge and awareness are necessary but not sufficient; people must also have motivation, enabling resources, and supportive social norms. Cultural beliefs and traditions shape hygiene behaviors, sometimes supporting them but at times discouraging practices like handwashing with soap. Social pressure and role modeling—seeing respected peers or community leaders practice good hygiene—can encourage adoption. Convenience and accessibility also determine behavior; if water and soap are not readily available, even motivated individuals may not wash hands regularly. Fear of disease can trigger short-term improvements in hygiene during outbreaks, but sustaining these behaviors requires reinforcement through habit formation and supportive environments. School-based hygiene education, community-led campaigns, and health promotion programs that integrate behavior change techniques—such as prompts, incentives, and public commitments—are effective at shifting habits.

Structural and environmental enablers are equally vital. Providing reliable water supply, ensuring continuous soap availability, and building user-friendly facilities remove physical barriers to hygiene. Integrating hygiene promotion into broader health, nutrition, and education programs increases reach and effectiveness. Monitoring behavior adoption and providing feedback also help maintain long-term change.

Hygiene practices are powerful yet behaviorally complex interventions for preventing disease. Their effectiveness depends not only on the presence of infrastructure and supplies but also on addressing the cognitive, social, and environmental factors that shape daily routines. Sustained improvements in public health require combining infrastructure development with behavioral strategies that make hygiene convenient, socially supported, and ingrained in daily life.

Infrastructure and Service Delivery Challenges

Infrastructure and service delivery challenges significantly hinder the effectiveness of WASH systems, undermining public health efforts and perpetuating the transmission of waterborne diseases. Reliable infrastructure is essential to provide safe drinking water, hygienic sanitation, and continuous access to hygiene facilities, yet many communities, particularly in low- and middle-income regions, face severe deficiencies. These challenges arise from inadequate investment, aging or poorly maintained systems, rapid population growth, urbanization, and governance gaps. Understanding these obstacles is vital to designing sustainable solutions that ensure equitable and resilient WASH services.

One of the primary challenges is inadequate coverage and access. Many rural areas lack basic water supply networks and sanitation facilities, forcing households to rely on unprotected wells, surface water, or open defecation, all of which increase exposure to pathogens. Urban informal settlements face different but equally severe challenges: dense populations often outpace the development of water and sanitation infrastructure, leading to overcrowded shared toilets, irregular water supply, and unsafe wastewater disposal. The lack of infrastructure coverage not only exposes people to unsafe environments but also limits their ability to practice essential hygiene behaviors like handwashing, contributing to persistent disease burdens.

Aging and poorly maintained infrastructure further compromise service reliability and water quality. Leaking or corroded pipes allow contaminants to enter water distribution systems, especially when water pressure drops. Intermittent supply, common in many low-resource settings, increases the risk of contamination during periods when empty pipes draw in polluted groundwater or sewage through cracks. Similarly, sanitation infrastructure such as pit latrines and septic tanks often overflow or leak when not properly maintained, contaminating soil and groundwater. These technical failures erode public trust in WASH systems, discourage usage, and create recurring public health hazards.

Financial constraints are a major barrier to building and sustaining WASH infrastructure. Many utilities and local governments operate with limited budgets, insufficient to cover capital investments, operation, maintenance, and staff training. This often results in deferred maintenance, poor service quality, and infrastructure that rapidly deteriorates. In some contexts, the lack of cost recovery through tariffs or user fees limits the ability of service providers to reinvest in their systems. External donor funding can support construction but often neglects the long-term operational financing needed to keep systems functional, leading to cycles of breakdown and abandonment.

Institutional and governance challenges compound these technical and financial barriers. Fragmented responsibilities among agencies can lead to gaps in planning, regulation, and accountability. Weak regulatory enforcement allows substandard construction and unsafe water quality to persist. Limited human resource capacity—especially trained engineers, technicians, and water quality specialists—further constrains service quality. In some regions, corruption and mismanagement undermine investment and reduce public confidence, discouraging households from paying for services or participating in community-led initiatives. Rapid urbanization and climate change add additional pressures, straining existing systems and increasing the frequency of floods, droughts, and contamination events.

Addressing infrastructure and service delivery challenges requires coordinated efforts to expand coverage, improve system resilience, and strengthen governance. This involves increasing investment in both hardware and long-term maintenance, enhancing regulatory oversight, building technical capacity, and fostering community participation to ensure services are sustainable and equitable. Without overcoming these challenges, WASH systems cannot effectively break the transmission of waterborne diseases or protect public health.

Chapter 4: Water-Related Vector-Borne and Parasitic Diseases

Water plays a central role in the transmission of vector-borne and parasitic diseases that continue to affect millions of people worldwide. Stagnant or poorly managed water sources create breeding grounds for mosquitoes and other vectors that spread malaria, dengue, and similar illnesses. Contaminated water is also a primary route for parasitic infections such as schistosomiasis and giardiasis, which impose heavy health burdens in many regions. Environmental changes, urbanization, and climate variability further influence the distribution and intensity of these diseases. This chapter explores the connections between water, vectors, and parasites, highlighting the health risks that arise from these interactions.

Ecology of Water-Related Disease Vectors

The ecology of water-related disease vectors plays a central role in shaping the transmission dynamics of many infectious diseases, particularly those caused by parasites, bacteria, and viruses that rely on intermediate hosts or vector species. Vectors are organisms, often insects or other invertebrates, that transmit pathogens from one host to another. In the context of water-related diseases, these vectors are intimately linked to aquatic or semi-aquatic environments at some stage of their life cycle. Understanding their ecological requirements, breeding habitats, population dynamics, and environmental drivers is essential to controlling their proliferation and reducing disease burdens.

Many of the most important water-related disease vectors are mosquitoes, which serve as primary carriers of pathogens responsible for malaria, dengue, chikungunya, Zika virus disease, and various forms of encephalitis. Mosquitoes depend on standing water for egg laying and larval development, and their population density is closely tied to the availability of suitable aquatic habitats. Species such as Anopheles (malaria vectors) prefer clean, sunlit pools and rice paddies, while Aedes (dengue and Zika vectors) thrive in small artificial containers like discarded tires, buckets, and cisterns. Culex species, which transmit West Nile virus and lymphatic filariasis, often breed in polluted water and stagnant drains. Temperature, rainfall, and humidity influence mosquito development rates, biting behavior, and survival. Warmer temperatures accelerate the extrinsic incubation period of pathogens inside mosquitoes, increasing transmission potential. Seasonal rains can produce large numbers of temporary water bodies, causing population surges that drive epidemic transmission.

Other key vectors include blackflies (Simulium species) that transmit onchocerciasis (river blindness). These flies breed exclusively in fast-flowing, oxygen-rich rivers and streams, attaching their larvae to submerged vegetation or rocks. Their distribution and abundance are strongly linked to river flow rates and water quality. Changes in river ecology from dam construction or water pollution can disrupt blackfly habitats, either suppressing or facilitating their proliferation. Similarly, freshwater snails act as intermediate hosts for schistosomes, the parasitic worms causing schistosomiasis. Snails such as Biomphalaria, Bulinus, and Oncomelania inhabit slow-moving or stagnant freshwater bodies including ponds, canals, and irrigation ditches. They release free-swimming larval forms (cercariae) that penetrate human skin on contact with contaminated water. Snail populations expand when aquatic vegetation is abundant and predators are scarce, conditions often created by agricultural water management, dam reservoirs, and poor drainage.

Environmental conditions and human activities exert strong control over vector ecology. Deforestation, irrigation projects, and urbanization can create or expand vector habitats by altering water flow, increasing surface water availability, and reducing natural predators. Rice cultivation, for example, provides ideal breeding sites for both Anopheles mosquitoes and schistosome-carrying snails. In urban areas, inadequate drainage, clogged gutters, and improper solid waste disposal produce numerous small water collections for Aedes mosquitoes. Climate variability and change further influence vector ecology by shifting temperature and precipitation patterns. Warmer temperatures can expand the geographic range of vectors to higher altitudes and latitudes, while altered rainfall patterns may produce either droughts that reduce breeding sites or heavy rains that generate new ones.

Socioeconomic conditions often exacerbate the ecological suitability of environments for vectors. Lack of piped water encourages households to store water in containers, which become breeding sites for Aedes mosquitoes if not properly covered. Inadequate sanitation leads to wastewater pooling and organic pollution that support Culex breeding. Unplanned urban growth can produce densely populated settlements with poor waste management, providing abundant vector habitats and facilitating rapid disease spread. These factors illustrate how human behaviors and infrastructure interact with ecological conditions to shape vector populations.

Effective control of water-related disease vectors requires addressing their ecological niches. Environmental management strategies aim to eliminate or modify breeding habitats, such as draining stagnant water, clearing vegetation from riverbanks, covering water storage containers, and improving solid waste management. Biological control methods include introducing predators like larvivorous fish or crustaceans to water bodies to reduce mosquito larvae or snail populations. Chemical interventions, such as larviciding and mollusciciding, can be targeted to known breeding sites, though they require careful application to avoid environmental harm and resistance development. Integrating these measures with improved water supply, sanitation infrastructure, and health education reduces both the availability of breeding habitats and human exposure to infectious vectors.

The ecology of water-related disease vectors demonstrates the complex interplay between environmental conditions, human activity, and pathogen transmission. Vectors thrive in specific aquatic habitats shaped by climate, hydrology, and land use, and their populations respond rapidly to ecological changes. Controlling water-related diseases therefore requires not only biomedical interventions but also ecological and environmental approaches that disrupt vector life cycles and minimize contact between vectors and humans. By addressing the ecological foundations of vector populations, public health strategies can more effectively reduce the transmission of water-related diseases and protect vulnerable communities.

Water-Associated Parasitic Infections

Water-associated parasitic infections are a major cause of morbidity and mortality globally, particularly in low- and middle-income regions where safe water, sanitation, and hygiene services are inadequate. These infections are caused by protozoa and helminths that depend on water either as a habitat for their intermediate stages or as a vehicle for transmission to humans. People become infected through ingestion of contaminated water or food, contact with contaminated water during domestic or occupational activities, or consumption of aquatic organisms carrying infective stages. The persistence of these parasites in the environment and their ability to reinfect human hosts make them particularly challenging to control.

Protozoan parasites are among the most common causes of waterborne disease. Giardia lamblia is a flagellated protozoan that infects the small intestine and causes giardiasis, a condition characterized by prolonged diarrhea, abdominal cramps, bloating, malabsorption, and weight loss. It is transmitted through ingestion of water contaminated with cysts shed in feces, often from humans or animals. Cryptosporidium parvum and Cryptosporidium hominis cause cryptosporidiosis, which leads to watery diarrhea, nausea, and abdominal pain. Cryptosporidium oocysts are highly resistant to chlorine disinfection and can survive for long periods in water, making them a major cause of outbreaks linked to drinking water and recreational water. Entamoeba histolytica, the agent of amoebiasis, spreads through ingestion of cysts in contaminated water or food and can cause dysentery, colitis, and liver abscesses. These protozoa are especially dangerous for children, as repeated or chronic infections can contribute to malnutrition and impaired cognitive development.

Free-living protozoa such as Naegleria fowleri and Acanthamoeba also pose risks when they contaminate warm freshwater environments. Naegleria fowleri causes primary amebic meningoencephalitis, a rare but almost universally fatal infection of the brain that occurs when contaminated water enters the nose during swimming or diving. Acanthamoeba can cause eye infections (keratitis) in contact lens users exposed to contaminated water. Although these infections are rare, their high fatality or complication rates make them significant public health concerns.

Several helminthic parasites rely on water for transmission. Schistosomes, the blood flukes that cause schistosomiasis, are among the most widespread water-associated helminths. Their larval stages are released from freshwater snails into contaminated water, where they penetrate human skin during activities such as swimming, fishing, or irrigation work. The worms mature in blood vessels, causing chronic inflammation and damage to the liver, intestines, bladder, and other organs. Schistosomiasis contributes to anemia, growth stunting, reduced work capacity, and, in severe cases, organ failure. Soil-transmitted helminths such as Ascaris lumbricoides, Trichuris trichiura, and hookworms are not directly waterborne but are often associated with environments where open defecation contaminates soil and water. Their eggs and larvae can be ingested via contaminated water or food, perpetuating cycles of infection.

Dracunculus medinensis, the Guinea worm, is another classic water-associated helminth. People become infected when they drink water containing tiny crustaceans (copepods) that carry the larvae. After about a year, adult female worms emerge from the skin, often on the lower limbs, causing painful ulcers. Although eradication efforts have drastically reduced Guinea worm disease, it illustrates how drinking water can act as a vector for helminth transmission. Other water-associated helminths include liver flukes (Clonorchis and Opisthorchis species) and intestinal flukes, which are transmitted through eating raw or undercooked freshwater fish or aquatic plants contaminated with infective larvae.

Environmental factors strongly influence the transmission of these parasitic infections. Warm temperatures, stagnant or slow-moving water, and poor sanitation create conditions conducive to parasite survival and spread. Flooding and inadequate wastewater management can contaminate surface water with parasite eggs and cysts. Agricultural practices such as wastewater irrigation can introduce parasites into food crops. Inadequate access to safe drinking water forces people to rely on contaminated sources, sustaining transmission cycles. Children are particularly vulnerable because of their frequent contact with soil and water and their developing immune systems.

Preventing water-associated parasitic infections requires integrated strategies addressing both environmental contamination and human exposure. Key measures include expanding access to safe water, improving sanitation infrastructure to prevent fecal contamination, and promoting hygiene practices such as handwashing and safe food handling. Water treatment methods like filtration, boiling, and chlorination can remove or inactivate many parasites, though resistant forms like Cryptosporidium require more advanced treatment such as ultraviolet disinfection. Controlling intermediate hosts, such as freshwater snails, through environmental management or biological control can reduce transmission of schistosomiasis. Public health education on the risks of untreated water, the importance of wearing protective clothing during water contact, and the need to thoroughly cook aquatic foods can also help break transmission cycles. Sustained investment and community engagement are essential to reducing the burden of these persistent and debilitating infections.

Environmental and Climatic Drivers of Disease Spread

Environmental and climatic factors play a pivotal role in shaping the transmission dynamics of water-related diseases, influencing the survival, reproduction, and distribution of pathogens and their vectors. Changes in temperature, precipitation, humidity, and land use directly affect water quality and availability, as well as the habitats of organisms that carry or host disease-causing agents.

These factors determine when and where outbreaks occur, how intense they become, and which populations are most at risk. Understanding these drivers is essential for predicting disease patterns and designing interventions to protect public health in a changing environment.

Temperature is a key climatic determinant of water-related disease transmission. Warmer temperatures accelerate the life cycles of many pathogens and vectors, increasing their reproduction and reducing the incubation period of diseases. For instance, higher temperatures can shorten the development time of Anopheles mosquitoes, which transmit malaria, and speed up the replication of viruses within mosquito hosts, enhancing transmission efficiency. Heat also promotes the proliferation of bacteria such as Vibrio cholerae in aquatic environments, increasing the risk of cholera outbreaks, especially in coastal and estuarine regions. Conversely, extremely high temperatures that dry up water bodies may reduce some vector populations, although this effect is often temporary and offset by the creation of new breeding habitats during subsequent rains.

Precipitation patterns strongly influence the availability and quality of water, thereby affecting disease risk. Heavy rainfall and flooding can overwhelm sanitation infrastructure, leading to the contamination of drinking water sources with fecal material. This facilitates the spread of waterborne pathogens such as Shigella, Salmonella, Escherichia coli, noroviruses, and rotaviruses, which cause diarrheal diseases. Floodwaters can also disperse Leptospira bacteria from the urine of infected animals into surface water, increasing the risk of leptospirosis. Standing water left after floods creates breeding habitats for mosquitoes, leading to surges in diseases such as malaria, dengue, and chikungunya. In contrast, drought conditions can concentrate pathogens in limited water sources, increase the use of unsafe water, and reduce hygiene practices due to water scarcity, thereby amplifying disease transmission.

Humidity influences pathogen and vector survival as well. High humidity prolongs the lifespan of mosquitoes and other insect vectors, allowing more time for them to acquire and transmit pathogens. It can also support the survival of certain bacterial and viral particles in the environment. Conversely, very low humidity can reduce the survival of airborne pathogens but often coincides with dry conditions that decrease water availability for hygiene, indirectly raising disease risk through poor sanitation practices.

Environmental modifications caused by human activity amplify these climatic effects. Deforestation, dam construction, irrigation schemes, and urban expansion alter hydrological patterns, often creating new habitats for vectors or disrupting ecosystems that naturally control them. Irrigation canals and rice paddies can support the proliferation of Anopheles mosquitoes and freshwater snails that transmit schistosomiasis. Urbanization often increases impermeable surfaces, leading to water pooling and poor drainage that support Aedes mosquitoes, which transmit dengue and Zika viruses. Informal settlements frequently lack adequate waste management, resulting in standing water contaminated with pathogens and organic matter that fosters vector breeding.

Climate change compounds these drivers by intensifying temperature extremes, altering rainfall regimes, and increasing the frequency and severity of extreme weather events. Rising sea surface temperatures and coastal flooding promote the spread of marine pathogens like Vibrio species. Expanding warm zones enable vectors and pathogens to colonize higher altitudes and latitudes, exposing new populations to diseases previously confined to tropical and subtropical regions. Changing climatic conditions also influence seasonal patterns, potentially extending transmission seasons and increasing the overall burden of disease.

The interaction of environmental and climatic drivers creates complex and dynamic disease landscapes. Communities with inadequate water, sanitation, and hygiene infrastructure are especially vulnerable because they have fewer buffers against these pressures. Strengthening surveillance systems, integrating climate and environmental data into disease forecasting, and improving water management and sanitation infrastructure are essential to reduce the health risks posed by environmental and climatic change. By addressing these underlying drivers, public health systems can better anticipate and mitigate the spread of water-related diseases in a rapidly changing world.

Control and Prevention Strategies

Control and prevention strategies for water-related diseases aim to break the transmission pathways of pathogens, reduce human exposure to contaminated water, and strengthen the systems that safeguard water quality. These strategies are most effective when implemented as part of an integrated approach that combines infrastructure development, behavior change, environmental management, and robust governance. Addressing the root causes of contamination and improving access to safe WASH are central to reducing the global burden of water-related illnesses.

Improving water quality is a cornerstone of disease prevention. This involves protecting water sources from contamination, treating water to remove pathogens, and maintaining the integrity of distribution systems. Source protection measures include preventing open defecation near water bodies, managing livestock access to water sources, and implementing watershed management to reduce runoff contamination. Effective treatment methods—such as filtration, chlorination, ultraviolet disinfection, and, for resistant pathogens, advanced membrane technologies—can eliminate microbial contaminants. Maintaining residual disinfectant levels in distribution systems helps prevent microbial regrowth and intrusion of contaminants through leaks or pressure fluctuations. Safe household water storage in clean, covered containers also reduces the risk of recontamination between collection and consumption.

Expanding and maintaining sanitation infrastructure is equally crucial. Safely managed sanitation systems prevent human waste from entering the environment and contaminating water sources.

This includes the construction and proper maintenance of toilets, septic systems, and sewer networks, as well as safe fecal sludge collection, transport, and treatment. In rural settings, low-cost technologies such as ventilated improved pit latrines can be effective, while urban areas often require more complex sewerage systems. Eliminating open defecation through community-led total sanitation programs helps reduce environmental contamination, lowering the risk of fecal-oral disease transmission.

Promoting hygiene practices complements water and sanitation infrastructure by reducing person-to-person and environment-to-person transmission of pathogens. Handwashing with soap at critical times, safe food handling, and hygienic care of children are proven to reduce diarrheal and respiratory infections. Behavior change interventions that combine education, social norms, and convenient access to handwashing facilities are essential to sustaining these practices. In healthcare and school settings, dedicated WASH infrastructure is vital for infection prevention and control, protecting both service users and staff.

Environmental management strategies can help control vector-borne water-related diseases. Draining stagnant water, clearing vegetation around water bodies, introducing larvivorous fish, and applying targeted larvicides can reduce vector populations. Managing irrigation systems and modifying dam operations can disrupt breeding habitats for mosquitoes and snails. Integrating these environmental measures with health interventions, such as mass drug administration for schistosomiasis, enhances their effectiveness and sustainability.

Strong governance, financing, and monitoring systems underpin all control and prevention efforts. Establishing and enforcing drinking water quality standards, investing in operation and maintenance, and building technical capacity are critical for long-term system performance. Surveillance systems that monitor water quality and disease incidence enable early detection of problems and rapid response to outbreaks. Public engagement and community participation are also vital to ensure acceptance, ownership, and sustainability of interventions.

Comprehensive control and prevention strategies that integrate safe water supply, adequate sanitation, good hygiene, environmental management, and effective governance are essential to reducing water-related disease burdens. By addressing the full chain of transmission, these strategies protect public health and contribute to sustainable development.

Chapter 5: Water Scarcity, Food Security, and Nutrition

Water scarcity is a growing global challenge that directly impacts food production, nutrition, and overall health. Agriculture accounts for the majority of freshwater use worldwide, and when water becomes limited, food systems suffer, leading to reduced crop yields, diminished livestock productivity, and increased food insecurity. These pressures contribute to malnutrition, stunted child development, and weakened immune systems, particularly in vulnerable communities. As climate change, population growth, and unsustainable water practices intensify scarcity, the links between water, food, and health become increasingly urgent. This chapter explores how water scarcity undermines nutrition and food security, and the resulting consequences for human health.

Water Scarcity and Its Implications for Health

Water scarcity is a growing global challenge with profound implications for human health. It occurs when the demand for water exceeds the available supply or when water quality is too poor to meet human and environmental needs. Scarcity can be physical, caused by insufficient natural water resources, or economic, resulting from inadequate infrastructure, governance, or financial capacity to deliver water. Climate change, population growth, urbanization, pollution, and unsustainable water use are intensifying scarcity in many regions. The health consequences are far-reaching, affecting hydration, nutrition, sanitation, hygiene, and the spread of diseases, as well as mental and social well-being.

One of the most direct health impacts of water scarcity is dehydration and its associated physiological stress. When clean drinking water is limited, individuals may consume less than required to maintain normal bodily functions, leading to impaired thermoregulation, reduced cognitive and physical performance, and increased risk of heat-related illnesses. Children, older adults, and people with chronic illnesses are particularly vulnerable. In arid and semi-arid regions where high temperatures coincide with water shortages, the risk of heat exhaustion, heat stroke, and kidney damage increases. Chronic low-level dehydration can also contribute to urinary tract infections and kidney stones, placing an additional burden on healthcare systems.

Water scarcity severely affects food security and nutrition, which are closely linked to health outcomes. Agriculture accounts for the largest share of global freshwater use, and limited water availability reduces crop yields, livestock productivity, and fisheries output. Droughts and depleted water supplies lead to food shortages, higher food prices, and reduced dietary diversity. This contributes to malnutrition, stunting, and weakened immune function, particularly in children. Poor water availability also affects the ability to produce and prepare safe food, increasing the risk of foodborne diseases. In regions dependent on subsistence farming, water scarcity can trigger cycles of poverty, hunger, and illness that perpetuate poor health across generations.

Hygiene and sanitation practices are heavily compromised under conditions of water scarcity, heightening the risk of infectious disease transmission. Limited water availability often forces households to prioritize drinking and cooking over hygiene activities such as handwashing, bathing, and cleaning. This can increase the spread of diarrheal diseases, respiratory infections, and skin and eye conditions. In healthcare settings, inadequate water for hand hygiene, cleaning, and disinfection undermines infection prevention and control, leading to higher rates of healthcare-associated infections. Similarly, schools without reliable water supplies struggle to maintain clean facilities, affecting student health and attendance, especially among girls during menstruation.

Scarcity also exacerbates the contamination of remaining water sources. As water volumes decline, pollutant concentrations increase, elevating exposure to pathogens, heavy metals, and chemical pollutants. Groundwater over-extraction can lead to the intrusion of saline water or arsenic into drinking water supplies, while reduced river flows can concentrate industrial and agricultural pollutants. Consuming contaminated water increases the risk of diarrheal diseases, cholera, typhoid, and other waterborne infections. These illnesses are particularly dangerous for children and immunocompromised individuals, further compounding the health burden in water-scarce areas.

Water scarcity has indirect but significant effects on mental health and social well-being. The daily stress of securing water, especially for women and girls who often bear the responsibility for water collection, contributes to anxiety, depression, and physical strain. Long journeys to fetch water can expose them to harassment and violence. Water-related conflicts over limited resources can also escalate tensions within and between communities, leading to displacement, injury, or loss of livelihoods. The disruption of education and income-generating activities due to water scarcity further undermines social stability and well-being, perpetuating cycles of vulnerability.

Climate change is amplifying water scarcity and its health impacts. Rising temperatures increase evapotranspiration and water demand, while altering precipitation patterns that disrupt river flows and groundwater recharge. Extreme weather events such as droughts and heatwaves are becoming more frequent and severe, intensifying competition for scarce water. As climate pressures grow, vulnerable populations face escalating health risks, including nutritional deficiencies, heat stress, disease outbreaks, and displacement linked to water insecurity.

Addressing the health implications of water scarcity requires comprehensive strategies that strengthen water security and build resilience. Expanding access to safe drinking water through improved infrastructure, sustainable groundwater management, and rainwater harvesting can reduce dehydration and disease risks. Increasing water-use efficiency in agriculture and promoting drought-resistant crops can enhance food security and nutrition. Integrating water supply with sanitation and hygiene programs ensures that limited water resources are used effectively to protect health. Climate adaptation measures, such as drought early warning systems and resilient water infrastructure, are critical to reducing health vulnerabilities. Community engagement, education, and governance reforms that promote equitable water allocation are also essential to safeguard health and well-being.

Water scarcity is not only an environmental or economic issue but a pressing public health challenge. Its impacts cascade through multiple pathways—physiological, nutritional, infectious, social, and psychological—undermining the foundations of health and development. Ensuring reliable access to sufficient, safe water is therefore essential to protecting human health and resilience in an increasingly water-stressed world.

Links Between Water Availability and Agricultural Production

Water availability is a fundamental determinant of agricultural production, shaping the quantity, quality, and stability of food supplies worldwide. Agriculture accounts for about 70 percent of global freshwater withdrawals, highlighting its dependence on reliable water resources for crop cultivation, livestock rearing, and aquaculture. The relationship between water and agriculture is complex and multidimensional: adequate water supports plant growth, nutrient uptake, soil health, and animal hydration, while water scarcity or variability can disrupt agricultural systems, reduce yields, and threaten food security. Understanding these links is crucial for managing water resources sustainably and ensuring resilient food systems in the face of growing demand and climate change.

Water is essential for plant physiological processes, including photosynthesis, nutrient transport, and cell turgor maintenance. Adequate soil moisture enables seeds to germinate, roots to absorb nutrients, and plants to develop leaves and fruits. Insufficient water disrupts these processes, leading to stunted growth, lower biomass accumulation, and reduced yields. Drought stress causes stomata to close to conserve water, limiting carbon dioxide uptake and reducing photosynthesis. Prolonged water deficits can result in plant wilting, leaf shedding, and reproductive failure. The timing of water availability is as important as its quantity—water stress during critical stages such as flowering or grain filling can cause significant yield losses even if total seasonal rainfall is near normal. Consistent and predictable water supplies are thus essential to maintain high and stable agricultural productivity.

Irrigation systems are a key means of ensuring water availability when rainfall is insufficient or unreliable. Irrigation allows farmers to grow crops in arid and semi-arid regions, extend growing seasons, and increase cropping intensity. It boosts yields, enables high-value crop production, and supports food security and rural livelihoods. However, irrigation also depends on the availability of freshwater from rivers, lakes, reservoirs, or aquifers, making it vulnerable to water scarcity and competition from other sectors. Over-extraction of groundwater for irrigation can deplete aquifers, lower water tables, and lead to land subsidence or saline intrusion. Surface water diversion can reduce downstream flows, harming ecosystems and other water users. Sustainable water allocation and efficient irrigation technologies, such as drip and sprinkler systems, are therefore essential to balance agricultural needs with long-term water resource protection.

Water availability also influences soil health, which is central to agricultural productivity. Adequate moisture supports the decomposition of organic matter, nutrient cycling, and microbial activity that maintain soil fertility. Water scarcity can cause soil to dry, compact, and lose structure, reducing its ability to hold nutrients and support plant roots. Repeated cycles of wetting and drying can lead to salinization in irrigated areas, as water evaporates and leaves salts behind. High soil salinity reduces plant water uptake and can render land unproductive. Proper water management, including controlled irrigation, drainage, and leaching, helps maintain soil quality and prevent salinity buildup, sustaining long-term productivity.

Livestock production is also directly tied to water availability. Animals require water for drinking, thermoregulation, and metabolic functions, while feed crops and pastures depend on water for growth. Water scarcity can reduce forage yields, lower pasture quality, and limit the availability of crop residues used as feed, thereby decreasing livestock productivity and reproduction rates. Drought can also increase animal disease risks by concentrating livestock around limited water points, facilitating the spread of pathogens. Inadequate water access forces herders to travel longer distances, leading to animal stress, weight loss, and mortality. Ensuring reliable water supplies for both animals and their feed sources is critical to maintaining livestock production systems.

Aquaculture and fisheries depend on sufficient water quantity and quality as well. Water supports the growth of aquatic organisms, maintains dissolved oxygen levels, and dilutes wastes. Reduced water availability can concentrate pollutants, lower oxygen levels, and raise water temperatures, stressing aquatic species and increasing disease outbreaks. Variability in water supply can disrupt breeding cycles and reduce harvests. Sustainable water management practices that maintain water flows, prevent contamination, and adapt to seasonal variability are vital to sustaining aquatic food production.

Climate change is intensifying the links between water availability and agricultural production by altering precipitation patterns, increasing temperatures, and increasing the frequency of droughts and floods. These changes affect water supplies for irrigation, degrade soil moisture, and disrupt planting and harvesting schedules. Farmers face growing uncertainty about water access, which undermines planning and increases the risk of crop failure and food insecurity. Building resilience requires improving water use efficiency, adopting drought- and flood-tolerant crop varieties, diversifying production systems, and integrating climate forecasting into water and farm management.

Water availability underpins every dimension of agricultural production—from plant growth and soil fertility to livestock and aquaculture systems. When water is abundant and well-managed, it drives productivity and food security; when scarce or unpredictable, it threatens livelihoods and nutrition. As demand for food and water grows alongside climate pressures, sustainable water management will be central to ensuring agricultural resilience and the stability of global food systems.

Water, Malnutrition, and Child Development

Water availability and quality are fundamental determinants of child health, nutrition, and development. Inadequate access to safe water contributes to a cascade of health challenges that undermine growth, cognitive development, and long-term well-being. Children are particularly vulnerable because their bodies and immune systems are still developing, and they have higher relative water needs than adults. The interplay between unsafe water, recurrent infections, and malnutrition creates a cycle that perpetuates poor health outcomes, impedes educational attainment, and increases the risk of mortality.

Unsafe water is a major cause of diarrheal diseases, which are closely linked to malnutrition. Pathogens such as Escherichia coli, Shigella, Rotavirus, and Cryptosporidium spread through contaminated drinking water and cause frequent bouts of diarrhea in young children. Each episode leads to loss of fluids, electrolytes, and nutrients, weakening the child's body and reducing appetite. Diarrhea also damages the intestinal lining, impairing nutrient absorption even after recovery. Repeated or chronic infections can cause environmental enteric dysfunction, a subclinical condition marked by intestinal inflammation and reduced absorptive capacity. This condition contributes to stunting, wasting, and micronutrient deficiencies that hinder physical and cognitive development. Children affected by stunting are more likely to experience delayed motor skills, poor school performance, and lower earning potential in adulthood.

Water scarcity also affects nutrition indirectly by limiting food production and dietary diversity. In many low-income regions, households rely on small-scale agriculture for food, and water shortages reduce crop yields and livestock productivity. This leads to seasonal food insecurity, decreased consumption of nutrient-rich foods such as fruits, vegetables, and animal products, and increased reliance on low-quality staples. The resulting deficiencies in protein, iron, zinc, vitamin A, and other essential nutrients compromise immune function and growth. Water scarcity further affects the ability to prepare and cook food safely, as inadequate water may force households to skip washing hands, utensils, or food, increasing the risk of contamination and foodborne illness. These combined factors reinforce the cycle of malnutrition and infection, both of which impair child development.

Poor water access undermines hygiene practices, further exacerbating malnutrition risks. Without sufficient water for handwashing and sanitation, fecal-oral transmission of pathogens becomes widespread. This continual exposure increases the burden of enteric infections and parasitic diseases such as soil-transmitted helminths and giardiasis, which consume nutrients from the host and cause intestinal inflammation. Chronic infections also divert energy and nutrients away from growth and development toward immune responses. Girls may face additional challenges if water scarcity limits their ability to manage menstruation hygienically, leading to school absenteeism and reduced educational opportunities that indirectly affect their long-term nutrition and health outcomes as future mothers.

The effects of inadequate water and malnutrition extend beyond physical growth to cognitive and psychosocial development. Malnourished children often show reduced attention spans, memory deficits, and slower learning, which can begin in early childhood and persist throughout life. Water-related illnesses and the fatigue associated with undernutrition reduce school attendance and participation, further constraining educational attainment. These developmental setbacks contribute to cycles of poverty and ill health that span generations, as malnourished girls are more likely to become malnourished mothers who give birth to low birth weight infants with higher risks of illness and developmental delays.

Breaking the links between unsafe water, malnutrition, and impaired child development requires integrated interventions. Ensuring universal access to safe drinking water reduces diarrheal disease and supports nutrient absorption. Pairing water supply improvements with sanitation infrastructure and hygiene promotion reduces exposure to enteric pathogens. Nutrition programs that provide micronutrient supplementation, breastfeeding support, and diverse diets complement WASH interventions to promote growth and development. School-based initiatives offering safe water, clean toilets, and hygiene education help improve attendance and health. Addressing these interconnected challenges through coordinated policies, investments, and community engagement is essential to safeguarding children's health and enabling them to reach their full developmental potential.

Integrated Water-Nutrition Interventions

Integrated water-nutrition interventions address the interconnected relationship between WASH, and nutrition to improve child health and development outcomes. These interventions recognize that efforts to combat undernutrition cannot succeed without simultaneously reducing exposure to waterborne pathogens and ensuring reliable access to safe water for drinking, food preparation, and hygiene. By combining WASH and nutrition strategies, integrated approaches disrupt the cycle in which poor water access contributes to infections, which in turn exacerbate malnutrition and impair growth. They are particularly critical in settings with high burdens of diarrheal disease, stunting, and food insecurity.

A key component of integrated interventions is improving access to safe drinking water. This reduces the incidence of diarrheal diseases and intestinal infections that contribute to nutrient loss and impaired absorption. Programs often include the construction or rehabilitation of community water supply systems, installation of household water treatment technologies such as filters or chlorination kits, and promotion of safe water storage practices to prevent recontamination. Reliable water access also enables households to diversify diets by supporting small-scale food production, such as vegetable gardens and poultry raising, which require water for irrigation and animal care. By reducing the time and energy spent collecting water, these interventions free caregivers—especially women—to focus more on child feeding and care.

Sanitation improvements are another core pillar. Safely managed sanitation systems, including latrines and fecal sludge management, prevent human waste from contaminating water sources and the household environment. Open defecation elimination campaigns, combined with community-led total sanitation approaches, reduce environmental exposure to fecal pathogens. This lowers the risk of chronic enteric infections and environmental enteric dysfunction, which can silently impair nutrient absorption and stunt growth even without overt diarrhea. When paired with nutrition interventions such as growth monitoring and micronutrient supplementation, sanitation improvements enhance the effectiveness of nutritional support by reducing the disease burden that undermines its benefits.

Hygiene promotion complements these measures by breaking the fecal-oral transmission pathway. Handwashing with soap at critical times—after defecation, before preparing food, and before feeding children—prevents the spread of pathogens that cause diarrhea and intestinal worms. Behavior change campaigns often use social marketing, visual cues, and community mobilization to build lasting habits. Improved hygiene practices protect the nutritional gains from feeding interventions, ensuring that nutrients are used for growth rather than diverted to fight infections. Nutrition education programs can be integrated with hygiene messaging to reinforce the importance of clean food preparation and feeding practices.

Integrated water-nutrition interventions are most effective when embedded within broader health and development systems. Linking WASH and nutrition services at clinics, schools, and community platforms ensures coordinated delivery and consistent messaging. Joint monitoring systems can track both WASH and nutrition indicators to assess impacts and guide adaptive management. Engaging local leaders and caregivers helps build ownership and sustain behavior change.

By addressing both the immediate and underlying causes of undernutrition, integrated water-nutrition interventions offer a holistic pathway to improving child survival, growth, and development, especially in vulnerable and resource-limited settings.

Chapter 6: Climate Change, Water Systems, and Health Impacts

Climate change is reshaping the availability, quality, and reliability of water resources, with profound consequences for human health. Shifts in rainfall patterns, rising temperatures, and the increasing frequency of extreme events such as floods, droughts, and storms disrupt water systems and expose populations to heightened risks. Contamination of drinking water, waterborne disease outbreaks, and reduced access to safe supplies are among the most pressing threats. Vulnerable groups, including children, the elderly, and low-income communities, are disproportionately affected. This chapter examines how climate change alters water systems and the resulting health impacts, highlighting pathways of vulnerability and resilience.

Climate Impacts on Water Availability and Quality

Climate change is exerting profound effects on both the availability and quality of water resources, reshaping hydrological systems and posing growing risks to public health, food security, and ecosystem integrity. Rising global temperatures, shifting precipitation patterns, accelerating glacier and snowpack melt, and the increasing frequency and intensity of extreme weather events are disrupting the natural water cycle. These changes are altering where, when, and how much water is available while simultaneously degrading its quality through heightened pollution, salinization, and pathogen proliferation. Understanding these climate-driven impacts is critical to developing strategies for safeguarding water security in a warming world.

One of the most visible impacts of climate change on water availability is the alteration of precipitation regimes. Many regions are experiencing shifts in rainfall patterns, with wetter areas often becoming wetter and drier regions becoming drier. In some parts of the world, rainfall is becoming more erratic and concentrated into intense events separated by longer dry periods. This variability undermines the reliability of surface water supplies, causing rivers, lakes, and reservoirs to experience both droughts and floods more frequently. Drought reduces streamflows and groundwater recharge, depleting water storage and forcing greater reliance on over-extracted aquifers. Prolonged droughts have already contributed to declining reservoir levels, reduced hydropower generation, and severe water shortages for agriculture and urban populations.

Melting glaciers and snowpacks further exacerbate water availability challenges. In many mountainous regions, glaciers and seasonal snow serve as natural water storage systems, releasing meltwater during warmer months when water demand is highest. Rising temperatures are accelerating glacier retreat and reducing snowpack accumulation, diminishing this crucial seasonal buffer. Initially, accelerated melting can increase river flows and flood risk, but over time, as ice reserves decline, it leads to reduced dry-season flows. This threatens water supplies for hundreds of millions of people who depend on glacier-fed rivers for drinking water, irrigation, and hydropower, especially in high mountain regions such as the Himalayas, Andes, and Alps.

Climate change also intensifies extreme weather events that disrupt water systems. More frequent and severe storms and floods can damage water infrastructure, overwhelm drainage and treatment systems, and contaminate water supplies with sediments, nutrients, heavy metals, and sewage. Conversely, heatwaves combined with drought can cause reservoirs to shrink and rivers to run dry, concentrating pollutants and reducing dilution capacity. Wildfires, which are becoming more frequent and intense under hotter, drier conditions, contribute large loads of ash, organic matter, and heavy metals to downstream waters, degrading water quality and complicating treatment processes.

Water quality is further affected by climate-driven changes in temperature and hydrology. Warmer water temperatures accelerate the growth of harmful microorganisms, including pathogenic bacteria and cyanobacteria (blue-green algae). Harmful algal blooms thrive in warm, nutrient-rich waters, producing toxins that contaminate drinking water and pose serious health risks. Increased evaporation during heatwaves can concentrate pollutants, while lower river flows during drought reduce the capacity of waterways to dilute and flush contaminants. Heavy rainfall events, meanwhile, increase surface runoff that carries fertilizers, pesticides, pathogens, and sediments into water bodies, degrading both surface and groundwater quality. Salinization is also intensifying in many coastal and arid regions as rising sea levels and reduced freshwater flows allow saltwater intrusion into coastal aquifers, rendering them unsuitable for drinking or irrigation without costly treatment.

These climate-related changes interact with human pressures such as population growth, land use change, and pollution, amplifying risks to water security. Water scarcity driven by climate stress increases competition among agriculture, industry, and domestic users, while declining water quality raises treatment costs and health risks. Vulnerable populations, especially in low-income and water-stressed regions, are most affected because they often lack resilient infrastructure, adaptive capacity, and financial resources to cope with climate impacts.

Adapting to climate-driven impacts on water availability and quality requires integrated water resource management that combines demand management, supply diversification, and ecosystem protection. Strategies include enhancing water-use efficiency in agriculture, expanding water storage through reservoirs and managed aquifer recharge, protecting watersheds to maintain natural filtration, and upgrading water treatment systems to handle new contamination challenges. Incorporating climate risk assessments into water planning, investing in resilient infrastructure, and strengthening monitoring systems are also crucial. By proactively addressing these challenges, societies can reduce vulnerability and build water systems that remain reliable and safe under changing climatic conditions.

Extreme Events and Waterborne Disease Outbreaks

Extreme weather events such as floods, hurricanes, cyclones, droughts, and heatwaves are becoming more frequent and intense due to climate change, and they have profound effects on the dynamics of waterborne disease outbreaks. These events disrupt water supply and sanitation infrastructure, alter environmental conditions that influence pathogen survival and transmission, and displace populations into conditions conducive to disease spread. The convergence of damaged infrastructure, contaminated water sources, and vulnerable human populations creates ideal conditions for outbreaks of diarrheal diseases, cholera, typhoid, leptospirosis, hepatitis A and E, and other waterborne infections. Understanding how extreme events drive these outbreaks is crucial to strengthening public health preparedness and resilience.

Floods are among the most significant drivers of waterborne disease outbreaks. When rivers overflow, storm surges inundate coastal areas, or heavy rains overwhelm drainage systems, floodwaters often mix with sewage, solid waste, animal feces, and industrial pollutants. This contamination spreads pathogenic bacteria, viruses, and parasites into surface and groundwater sources used for drinking, cooking, and washing. Flood conditions also disrupt water treatment facilities and damage distribution networks, reducing or eliminating disinfection and allowing pathogens to enter piped water systems. Standing water left after floods provides breeding grounds for disease vectors such as mosquitoes, further compounding public health risks. Flood-related outbreaks often include cholera, leptospirosis, dysentery, and hepatitis E, with the risk heightened in densely populated areas lacking adequate sanitation and drainage infrastructure.

Hurricanes and cyclones can produce similar health impacts through storm surges, extreme rainfall, and infrastructure destruction. High winds and flooding can contaminate water supplies, disable pumping and treatment systems, and rupture sewage networks, leading to widespread mixing of wastewater with potable water. Power outages interrupt chlorination and other treatment processes, while debris and damage impede water delivery and sanitation services. Following such storms, crowded emergency shelters often have inadequate water and sanitation facilities, facilitating person-to-person and environmental transmission of waterborne diseases. Displacement and disrupted healthcare access exacerbate these risks, delaying outbreak detection and response. Past disasters, such as the surge in cholera cases after Haiti's 2010 earthquake compounded by Hurricane Hurricane Tomas, illustrate how extreme events can trigger prolonged waterborne disease crises in vulnerable settings.

Droughts also contribute to waterborne disease outbreaks, though through different mechanisms. Reduced rainfall lowers river flows and groundwater recharge, concentrating pathogens and pollutants in shrinking water sources. As surface water becomes scarce, communities may resort to using unsafe sources such as unprotected wells, ponds, or contaminated storage containers. Limited water availability reduces hygiene practices like handwashing and cleaning, increasing the risk of fecal-oral disease transmission. Drought can also compromise water treatment by reducing raw water quality and volume, while stagnant conditions favor the persistence of pathogens. These factors increase the incidence of diarrheal diseases, hepatitis A, and other infections during prolonged dry periods, especially where infrastructure and water governance are weak.

Heatwaves and rising temperatures further amplify waterborne disease risks by affecting pathogen ecology and water quality. Warmer water accelerates the growth of bacteria such as Vibrio cholerae and Legionella, and promotes harmful algal blooms that release toxins and create environments favorable to microbial proliferation. High temperatures can also reduce dissolved oxygen levels and concentrate pollutants as water volumes decline, increasing the likelihood of contamination and illness. Heat-related water scarcity can indirectly elevate disease risks by limiting hygiene practices and forcing reliance on marginal water sources. In coastal areas, warm sea surface temperatures combined with flooding events can spark outbreaks of Vibrio-related infections, which are particularly dangerous for immunocompromised individuals.

The health impacts of extreme event–driven outbreaks are magnified by population displacement, infrastructure disruption, and healthcare system strain. Disasters often force people into temporary shelters or camps with overcrowding, poor sanitation, and limited clean water access, creating ideal conditions for explosive transmission of waterborne pathogens. Damaged transportation networks and health facilities delay outbreak detection, response, and treatment. Public health surveillance systems may be disrupted just as the need for rapid data and coordinated interventions becomes critical. Vulnerable populations, including children, older adults, and people in low-income or informal settlements, bear the greatest burden due to preexisting health inequities and limited access to healthcare.

Mitigating the risk of waterborne disease outbreaks during extreme events requires proactive, integrated strategies. Strengthening water and sanitation infrastructure to withstand floods, storms, and power outages reduces contamination risks. Establishing emergency water supply and treatment systems, such as mobile filtration and chlorination units, ensures access to safe water during crises. Pre-positioning hygiene supplies, deploying rapid water quality monitoring, and training local health workers improve outbreak detection and response capacity. Integrating WASH interventions into disaster preparedness plans, alongside early warning systems and climate risk assessments, can reduce vulnerability. Community education on safe water handling, hygiene, and sanitation during emergencies also helps prevent disease spread.

Extreme events are intensifying under climate change, and their intersection with waterborne disease transmission represents a growing threat to public health. By reinforcing water systems, strengthening emergency preparedness, and integrating health and WASH responses, societies can reduce the likelihood and severity of waterborne disease outbreaks that follow these disruptive events.

Vulnerability of Health Systems to Climate-Water Risks

Health systems are increasingly vulnerable to the complex and intensifying risks posed by the interaction of climate change and water insecurity. Climate-driven changes—such as more frequent floods, droughts, heatwaves, and storms—are disrupting water supply and sanitation infrastructure, degrading water quality, and altering the distribution of water-related diseases. These impacts strain health systems by increasing patient loads, damaging critical infrastructure, and disrupting the supply chains and workforce needed to deliver care. Many health systems, particularly in low- and middle-income countries, already operate with limited resources and are poorly equipped to manage the escalating pressures created by climate-water risks.

One of the primary vulnerabilities lies in the physical infrastructure of health facilities. Many hospitals and clinics depend on reliable water supplies for drinking, cleaning, sanitation, sterilization, and cooling. Extreme events such as floods can damage or destroy water supply networks, contaminate water sources with sewage and debris, and disable treatment plants, leaving health facilities without safe water during periods of heightened disease risk. Droughts can similarly reduce water availability, forcing facilities to ration or suspend essential hygiene practices like handwashing and surface disinfection. Heatwaves increase water demand for cooling systems while reducing water availability, threatening the operation of laboratories, intensive care units, and other heat-sensitive equipment. Facilities built in floodplains, coastal zones, or areas with aging infrastructure are especially exposed to climate-related water disruptions.

Water-related disease surges triggered by climate extremes further stress health systems by overwhelming service capacity. Flooding and heavy rainfall often precipitate outbreaks of diarrheal diseases, cholera, leptospirosis, and hepatitis A and E, while drought conditions increase the risk of diarrheal and parasitic infections due to poor hygiene and use of contaminated sources. Warmer temperatures and changing rainfall patterns can expand the range and seasonality of vector-borne diseases such as malaria and dengue, increasing patient numbers and straining diagnostic and treatment services. When outbreaks occur, health systems may face sudden surges in demand for care, isolation capacity, and medical supplies at the same time they are coping with damaged infrastructure and disrupted water access.

Health workforce capacity is another critical vulnerability. Extreme events can displace or endanger healthcare workers, damage their homes, and block transportation routes, reducing staff availability during emergencies. Waterborne disease outbreaks can increase occupational exposure risks for staff working without adequate water for hygiene and infection prevention. Prolonged crises can lead to burnout, attrition, and reduced workforce resilience, weakening the system's ability to respond to future shocks. In many settings, shortages of trained personnel already limit routine health service delivery, leaving little surge capacity to handle climate-related health emergencies.

Weak governance, financing, and supply chain systems compound these vulnerabilities. Health systems often lack contingency plans, risk assessments, or dedicated funding to prepare for and respond to climate-water hazards. Disasters can disrupt supply chains for water treatment chemicals, hygiene products, and medical supplies, hampering both patient care and infection prevention measures. Limited surveillance and data integration reduce the ability to detect and respond rapidly to water-related disease outbreaks. These systemic weaknesses can turn climate-water shocks into cascading health crises that extend far beyond the initial event.

Building resilience requires mainstreaming climate and water risk management into health system planning and operations. This includes designing and retrofitting health facilities to withstand floods, storms, and heat, while ensuring reliable backup water supplies and treatment systems. Strengthening WASH infrastructure in healthcare facilities is essential to maintain infection control during crises. Training health workers in climate and water risk response, establishing early warning and surveillance systems, and developing emergency preparedness plans can enhance response capacity. Adequate financing mechanisms, supply chain diversification, and intersectoral coordination are also critical to sustain services during disruptions.

Health systems sit on the front lines of climate and water challenges, yet many remain highly vulnerable to their combined impacts. Addressing these vulnerabilities through infrastructure resilience, workforce support, governance reform, and integrated WASH measures is vital to protect population health and ensure continuity of care in an increasingly climate-uncertain world.

Building Climate-Resilient Water and Health Systems

Building climate-resilient water and health systems is essential to protect populations from the escalating impacts of climate change on water security and public health. Climate change intensifies extreme weather events, disrupts water supplies, degrades water quality, and shifts the distribution of water-related diseases. Health systems depend on reliable WASH services to prevent disease transmission, maintain infection control, and deliver safe care. When climate shocks compromise water systems, they simultaneously weaken health system functionality. Resilience-building involves strengthening infrastructure, governance, workforce capacity, and community engagement to anticipate, absorb, and recover from climate-water risks while continuing to deliver essential health services.

A critical component of climate resilience is upgrading water infrastructure to withstand climate extremes. This includes climate-proofing water supply systems by diversifying sources—such as combining surface water, groundwater, and rainwater harvesting—so that if one source fails, others can meet demand. Designing storage and distribution networks to withstand floods, droughts, and temperature extremes ensures continuous access to safe water. Protecting water sources through watershed conservation, pollution control, and land-use planning reduces contamination risks during storms and floods. Embedding climate risk assessments into water system design helps anticipate future stressors, allowing infrastructure to be located, sized, and managed to remain functional under shifting conditions.

Strengthening health systems requires parallel investments in resilient WASH services within healthcare facilities. Clinics and hospitals need secure water supply systems, backup storage, on-site treatment capacity, and reliable sanitation to maintain infection prevention and control during crises. Facilities should be sited and built to withstand floods, storms, and heatwaves, with elevated platforms, protected water storage, and climate-responsive ventilation and cooling. Contingency plans must include protocols for maintaining water quality, disinfection, and hygiene when supply disruptions occur. These measures ensure that health facilities remain operational during climate shocks, protecting both patients and health workers from water-related infections.

Resilient systems also depend on strong governance, financing, and workforce capacity. Water and health sectors must coordinate to jointly plan for climate risks, align policies, and mobilize resources. Establishing dedicated funding streams for climate adaptation in water and health ensures that infrastructure improvements, maintenance, and emergency response capacities are sustained over time. Training health workers in climate-related disease surveillance, risk communication, and emergency WASH measures enhances their capacity to respond to outbreaks triggered by floods, droughts, or heatwaves. Cross-sector emergency preparedness plans should integrate WASH and health response strategies, including rapid deployment of water treatment, hygiene supplies, and mobile clinics during disasters.

Community engagement is essential to sustain climate resilience. Local participation in water resource management, health promotion, and disaster preparedness builds trust, ensures that interventions are culturally appropriate, and mobilizes local knowledge. Early warning systems that link climate and health data can alert communities and facilities to impending hazards, enabling proactive measures such as stockpiling water treatment chemicals, reinforcing infrastructure, and scaling up health outreach.

Building climate-resilient water and health systems requires coordinated, multisectoral action that integrates infrastructure improvements, governance reform, workforce strengthening, and community-based preparedness. By reinforcing the foundations of safe water and robust healthcare, these systems can withstand climate shocks, protect health during crises, and support long-term sustainable development.

Chapter 7: Water Infrastructure and Health System Resilience

Reliable water infrastructure is essential for maintaining public health and ensuring that healthcare systems function effectively. Safe water supplies, wastewater treatment, and resilient distribution networks provide the foundation for preventing disease and protecting communities from outbreaks. When infrastructure fails or is disrupted, health systems face increased pressure, with hospitals, clinics, and households unable to maintain adequate hygiene or ensure safe drinking water. Aging systems, climate-related risks, and inadequate investments further increase vulnerabilities. This chapter explores the connections between water infrastructure and health resilience, examining how robust systems support both everyday needs and emergency preparedness.

Safe Water Supply in Healthcare Facilities

Safe water supply in healthcare facilities is essential for ensuring quality care, preventing healthcare-associated infections, and protecting the health of patients, staff, and visitors. Water is required for drinking, preparing food and medications, cleaning medical instruments, maintaining personal and environmental hygiene, and supporting sanitation systems. When water supplies are unsafe, unreliable, or unavailable, healthcare services are compromised, infection prevention and control break down, and the risk of disease transmission increases. This makes safe water supply a cornerstone of resilient, effective, and equitable health systems.

Healthcare facilities need reliable access to water of adequate quantity and quality for all operational needs. Safe water must be microbiologically clean, free from harmful chemicals, and acceptable in taste, odor, and appearance. The WHO recommends that healthcare facilities provide at least 5 liters of safe water per outpatient per day, 40–60 liters per inpatient per day, and higher amounts in specialized wards such as maternity and surgical units. Water quality should meet national drinking water standards or, where unavailable, WHO guidelines. This includes the absence of detectable Escherichia coli or thermotolerant coliforms in 100 mL of water and adequate residual chlorine to prevent microbial regrowth in distribution systems. Regular monitoring is essential to ensure compliance, especially during periods of system disruption.

Safe water supply systems must be designed to ensure both continuous availability and protection from contamination. Facilities should have secure access to an improved water source, such as a piped network, borehole, or protected well, with sufficient yield throughout the year. Where piped water is used, backflow prevention devices and regular maintenance are needed to prevent contamination from cross-connections or pressure losses. Water should be stored in covered, clean tanks to buffer against supply interruptions and provide reserves during peak demand or emergencies. Storage infrastructure should be elevated or protected from flooding to prevent ingress of surface contaminants. On-site disinfection, typically chlorination, is critical to maintaining water safety, particularly in settings where source water quality is variable or unreliable.

Healthcare facilities also need reliable internal distribution systems to deliver water to all points of care. Piping networks should be designed to ensure adequate pressure and avoid dead-ends or stagnant zones where microbial growth can occur. Regular inspection and flushing of systems help prevent biofilm accumulation and Legionella growth, especially in large or complex buildings. Plumbing systems should clearly separate potable water from non-potable supplies used for equipment cooling, firefighting, or irrigation to prevent cross-contamination. Hot water systems should be maintained at temperatures that limit microbial proliferation, with mixing valves installed to prevent scalding.

Contingency measures are essential to maintain safe water during supply disruptions. Facilities should have emergency water storage sufficient for at least 48–72 hours of operation and plans to secure alternative water sources, such as tankered deliveries or portable treatment units, during crises. Regular drills and clear roles for staff enhance preparedness. Mobile disinfection systems and point-of-use treatment, such as filtration or ultraviolet disinfection, can provide rapid protection when water quality is compromised. Backup power supplies are necessary to operate pumps and treatment systems during outages.

Institutional arrangements and governance are crucial for sustaining safe water in healthcare facilities. Responsibilities for water safety must be clearly assigned within facility management, supported by adequate budgets, staff training, and maintenance plans. Water safety plans, as recommended by WHO, provide a risk-based framework for assessing hazards, implementing control measures, and monitoring performance from source to point of use. Coordination with local water utilities and public health authorities supports rapid response to contamination events and infrastructure failures.

Safe water supply in healthcare facilities underpins infection prevention, patient safety, and service continuity. Ensuring reliable access requires robust infrastructure, proactive management, and preparedness for emergencies. Strengthening water systems within healthcare settings is therefore fundamental to building resilient health systems capable of protecting lives during both routine operations and climate-related shocks.

Aging Infrastructure and Health Risks

Aging water infrastructure poses significant risks to public health, particularly within healthcare facilities where safe water is essential for patient care, infection prevention, and sanitation. As water supply systems, plumbing networks, and treatment facilities deteriorate over time, their ability to deliver safe and reliable water declines. Cracked pipes, corroded fixtures, leaking storage tanks, and malfunctioning treatment components can allow contaminants to enter water systems or compromise disinfection processes. These failures increase the risk of waterborne disease outbreaks, healthcare-associated infections, and chemical exposures, threatening both patient safety and the broader community.

One of the most serious health risks associated with aging infrastructure is microbial contamination. Old pipes often develop cracks, leaks, or loose joints that allow pathogens to enter through infiltration, especially when water pressure drops or intermittent supply creates negative pressure. Contaminated groundwater or wastewater can be drawn into damaged sections of distribution systems, introducing bacteria, viruses, and protozoa. Biofilms—complex microbial communities that form on the inner surfaces of aging pipes—harbor pathogens such as Legionella, Pseudomonas, and nontuberculous mycobacteria. These organisms can detach from biofilms and enter tap water, where they pose serious risks to immunocompromised patients. Aging hot water systems in particular are prone to Legionella proliferation if temperatures are not consistently maintained above levels that inhibit bacterial growth, potentially causing outbreaks of Legionnaires' disease.

Chemical contamination is another concern linked to deteriorating infrastructure. Corrosion of old pipes and fixtures can release metals such as lead, copper, and iron into drinking water. Chronic exposure to lead, even at low levels, can cause neurological damage, developmental delays, and behavioral problems in children, as well as cardiovascular and kidney effects in adults. Copper leaching can cause gastrointestinal distress and, at high levels, liver and kidney damage. Corroded pipes can also react with disinfectants, reducing residual chlorine levels needed to control microbial growth and producing harmful disinfection by-products. The presence of rust and sediment from aging infrastructure can shield pathogens from disinfection, further undermining water safety.

Intermittent supply, low water pressure, and leaks caused by infrastructure deterioration create conditions that increase contamination risks. Aging systems often experience frequent pipe bursts and pressure fluctuations, which not only disrupt service but also draw in pollutants through cracks and breaks. Water loss from leaks reduces system efficiency and can lead to stagnation in parts of the network, providing ideal conditions for microbial growth. Healthcare facilities are especially vulnerable because interruptions or contamination can compromise infection prevention measures, endangering vulnerable patients and increasing the risk of healthcare-associated infections.

Aging infrastructure also impedes effective monitoring and maintenance. Old systems may lack modern design features such as access points for sampling, automated sensors, or clear mapping of buried components, making it difficult to detect contamination, locate leaks, or assess system integrity. Deferred maintenance, often due to budget constraints, accelerates deterioration and increases the likelihood of sudden failures. When breakdowns occur, emergency repairs may be delayed by a lack of spare parts or technical expertise, prolonging service disruptions and health risks.

Addressing the health risks posed by aging water infrastructure requires proactive assessment, investment, and governance. Comprehensive infrastructure audits can identify vulnerable components, prioritize replacements, and guide preventive maintenance plans. Rehabilitating or replacing old pipes, fixtures, tanks, and treatment systems reduces contamination pathways and improves reliability. Implementing corrosion control measures, maintaining adequate disinfectant residuals, and flushing stagnant sections of the network can mitigate risks while long-term upgrades are underway. Establishing asset management systems helps track infrastructure condition, schedule maintenance, and allocate budgets effectively. In healthcare settings, water safety plans should incorporate infrastructure risk assessments, routine monitoring, and contingency measures for supply interruptions or contamination events.

Aging infrastructure is an often-overlooked but critical threat to water safety and public health. Its deterioration increases the likelihood of microbial and chemical contamination, system failures, and service disruptions. Proactively upgrading and maintaining water systems is essential to protect health, ensure reliable water delivery, and support the safe functioning of healthcare facilities and communities.

Digital Monitoring and Water Safety Management

Digital monitoring has emerged as a transformative tool for strengthening water safety management, offering real-time insights into water quality, system performance, and potential risks. Traditional water safety management often relies on periodic sampling and manual inspections, which can leave gaps in surveillance and delay responses to contamination events. Digital systems, by contrast, enable continuous monitoring, rapid data analysis, and early detection of hazards, allowing water utilities and healthcare facilities to proactively manage risks and safeguard public health. Integrating digital technologies into water safety plans enhances both operational efficiency and resilience to climate and infrastructure challenges.

A key component of digital water safety management is the use of sensor-based monitoring networks. Online sensors can continuously measure critical water quality parameters such as turbidity, pH, temperature, residual chlorine, conductivity, and dissolved oxygen. Advanced sensors can detect specific contaminants, including heavy metals, nitrates, and microbial indicators. These devices are deployed at strategic points along the water supply chain—from source water and treatment plants to distribution systems and points of use—providing real-time data on system conditions. This constant flow of information allows operators to detect anomalies such as sudden turbidity spikes or disinfectant residual drops, which can indicate contamination or treatment failures, and respond before water reaches users.

Supervisory Control and Data Acquisition (SCADA) systems form the backbone of many digital monitoring frameworks. SCADA platforms collect data from sensors, pumps, valves, and other equipment, transmitting it to centralized control rooms where operators can visualize system status, adjust operations, and receive alerts. By automating data collection and control, SCADA systems reduce human error and enable rapid responses to changing conditions. They can trigger automatic shutdowns, rerouting of water flows, or activation of backup disinfection systems when problems are detected, minimizing the risk of contaminated water entering distribution networks.

Digital platforms also enable predictive analytics for risk management. Machine learning algorithms can analyze historical and real-time data to identify patterns that precede contamination events or infrastructure failures. For example, correlations between rainfall intensity, turbidity increases, and microbial detections can be used to forecast contamination risks during storms. Predictive models can also estimate the likelihood of pipe bursts, leaks, or corrosion based on pressure fluctuations and flow anomalies, helping prioritize preventive maintenance. These tools shift water safety management from reactive to proactive, reducing the likelihood and impact of system failures.

Integrating digital monitoring with water safety plans enhances their effectiveness. Water safety plans, promoted by the World Health Organization, use a risk-based approach to identify hazards, assess risks, and implement control measures from source to tap. Digital systems support this approach by providing continuous verification that control measures are functioning and by enabling rapid corrective actions when risks emerge. Data from digital monitoring can also feed into regulatory reporting, performance benchmarking, and public transparency platforms, strengthening accountability and trust.

Cybersecurity and data governance are critical considerations as water systems become increasingly digitized. Unauthorized access, data manipulation, or system disruptions could compromise both safety and service continuity. Robust cybersecurity measures, including encryption, firewalls, user authentication, and regular system audits, are essential to protect digital monitoring infrastructure. Clear protocols for data management, privacy, and ownership ensure that information is accurate, secure, and appropriately used.

Digital monitoring offers powerful tools for improving water safety management, but its success depends on enabling infrastructure, trained personnel, and sustained investment. Facilities must ensure reliable power supplies, stable internet connectivity, and routine calibration and maintenance of sensors. Staff require training in digital system operation, data interpretation, and emergency response procedures. Financing mechanisms should support both capital costs and long-term operational budgets to prevent technology obsolescence or neglect.

By providing real-time data, predictive insights, and automated control, digital monitoring systems strengthen the ability of water providers and healthcare facilities to detect risks early, respond swiftly, and maintain safe water supplies. Embedding these tools within water safety management frameworks enhances public health protection and builds resilience to the growing challenges of aging infrastructure, population growth, and climate variability.

Strengthening Governance for Health-Resilient Infrastructure

Water infrastructure plays a vital role in safeguarding public health. From the treatment and distribution of drinking water to the collection and treatment of wastewater, robust systems are necessary to protect populations from disease and ensure reliable access to safe water. However, infrastructure alone cannot guarantee health security. Governance—the policies, regulations, institutions, and accountability mechanisms that guide decision-making and management—forms the backbone of health-resilient water systems. Strengthening governance is therefore essential to ensure infrastructure investments deliver long-term, equitable, and sustainable health outcomes.

A central aspect of governance is the establishment of clear regulatory frameworks. Effective laws and regulations define water quality standards, enforce compliance, and establish accountability for both public and private service providers. Without strong enforcement, even advanced infrastructure may fail to protect health, as lapses in monitoring or maintenance can compromise water safety. Regulatory systems must also evolve with emerging challenges such as climate change, urbanization, and new contaminants. Adaptive governance, which regularly reviews and updates regulations, helps ensure that infrastructure remains resilient to current and future risks.

Institutional coordination is another key component. Water infrastructure intersects with multiple sectors, including health, environment, and urban development. Fragmented responsibilities can lead to inefficiencies, duplication, or gaps in service delivery. Strong governance frameworks encourage cross-sectoral collaboration, ensuring that infrastructure planning integrates health priorities alongside technical and financial considerations. For example, coordination between ministries of health and water utilities can align water safety planning with disease surveillance, creating early warning systems for waterborne outbreaks.

Financing mechanisms also require robust governance. Infrastructure development and maintenance are capital-intensive, and without sustainable funding models, systems risk degradation. Transparent financial governance ensures that resources are mobilized, allocated, and spent effectively. This includes establishing tariffs that balance affordability with cost recovery, leveraging public-private partnerships responsibly, and directing subsidies toward vulnerable populations. Equitable financing helps prevent service inequalities that can exacerbate health disparities, particularly in marginalized communities.

Community engagement and accountability mechanisms strengthen governance by making infrastructure systems more inclusive and responsive. Involving local populations in planning and oversight fosters trust, improves service uptake, and ensures that infrastructure meets community needs. Mechanisms such as citizen report cards, grievance redress systems, and participatory budgeting enhance transparency and accountability, reducing the risk of corruption and mismanagement. Moreover, when communities are engaged, they are more likely to contribute to infrastructure maintenance and adopt safe water practices that support health resilience.

Another dimension is the integration of risk management into governance systems. Health-resilient infrastructure must be designed and operated with consideration for hazards such as floods, droughts, and contamination events. Governance frameworks should mandate risk assessments, emergency response protocols, and contingency planning for critical infrastructure. This proactive approach reduces vulnerabilities and ensures continuity of essential services during crises. Climate adaptation strategies—such as protecting source watersheds, diversifying water supplies, and upgrading treatment capacity—should be embedded in governance processes to build long-term resilience.

Governance must also prioritize equity and inclusion. Vulnerable groups—including women, children, the elderly, and those in low-income or marginalized communities—often bear the greatest health risks from inadequate water infrastructure. Policies that explicitly recognize the human right to water and health help safeguard these groups. Inclusive governance ensures that infrastructure investments target underserved populations, narrowing inequalities and strengthening societal resilience as a whole.

Chapter 8: Socioeconomic Inequalities, Water Access, and Health

Socioeconomic factors strongly shape how individuals and communities access water, creating disparities that translate into unequal health outcomes. Income levels, education, employment opportunities, and social status influence the availability, affordability, and quality of water services. Wealthier households are more likely to secure reliable and safe supplies, while low-income and marginalized groups often depend on unsafe or inconsistent sources. These inequities deepen cycles of vulnerability, as poor health further limits economic opportunities. This chapter examines how socioeconomic inequalities affect water access and health, highlighting the ways in which poverty, exclusion, and structural barriers reinforce disparities across populations.

Water Inequities and Health Disparities

Access to safe and reliable water services is a fundamental determinant of health, yet inequities in water availability, affordability, and quality continue to produce disparities across populations. These inequities often stem from geographic, economic, and social divides, leading to unequal health outcomes. Communities that face persistent water insecurity are more vulnerable to disease, malnutrition, and environmental hazards, reinforcing cycles of poverty and disadvantage. Examining the link between water inequities and health disparities reveals the urgent need to address both structural barriers and social determinants to achieve equitable health outcomes for all.

Geographic disparities in water access play a central role in shaping health outcomes. Urban areas often benefit from centralized water infrastructure, while rural and peri-urban communities may rely on unsafe or unreliable sources. In many regions, marginalized populations are forced to draw water from rivers, ponds, or unprotected wells, exposing them to microbial and chemical contaminants. This uneven distribution of infrastructure results in higher incidences of diarrheal diseases, parasitic infections, and other waterborne illnesses in underserved areas. Furthermore, geographic isolation can hinder timely responses to contamination events, prolonging exposure and exacerbating health risks.

Economic inequities further compound water-related health disparities. The cost of accessing safe water varies widely across contexts, and low-income households often spend a disproportionate share of their income on water. In some urban settings, residents of informal settlements pay more per unit of water from vendors than wealthier households connected to municipal systems. High costs can force households to ration water, leading to inadequate hygiene practices and increased vulnerability to disease transmission. Economic inequities also affect the ability of communities to invest in infrastructure improvements or maintenance, perpetuating cycles of unsafe water and poor health.

Social inequities, including those related to gender, ethnicity, and age, intersect with water access to deepen health disparities. Women and girls in many societies bear the responsibility of collecting water, often traveling long distances under unsafe conditions. The time spent fetching water reduces opportunities for education and employment, reinforcing gender inequalities. Moreover, the physical burden of water collection contributes to musculoskeletal injuries and fatigue, while exposure to unsafe sources heightens health risks. Minority groups and indigenous populations are frequently excluded from decision-making processes regarding water governance, leaving them with inadequate services and heightened exposure to contaminated water sources. Vulnerable groups such as children and the elderly face greater health impacts due to weaker immune systems and increased susceptibility to waterborne pathogens.

The health consequences of water inequities are broad and severe. Lack of access to safe drinking water is a leading cause of diarrheal diseases, which disproportionately affect children under five and remain a major cause of preventable deaths. Water scarcity contributes to poor sanitation and hygiene, facilitating the spread of diseases such as cholera, typhoid, and dysentery. Inadequate water services also compromise maternal and child health by increasing risks of infection during childbirth and hindering proper nutrition through reduced agricultural productivity. Chronic exposure to contaminated water sources, particularly those polluted with arsenic, fluoride, or industrial chemicals, leads to long-term health problems including cancers, neurological damage, and developmental disorders.

Climate change exacerbates these inequities by intensifying water scarcity, flooding, and contamination. Poorer communities are often less equipped to cope with climate-related water challenges, facing greater health risks during droughts, storms, and extreme weather events. Rising competition for water resources can also deepen inequities, as powerful groups secure access at the expense of marginalized populations. Without deliberate policies to address vulnerabilities, climate change threatens to widen health disparities linked to water access and quality.

Addressing water inequities and the resulting health disparities requires targeted interventions that prioritize inclusion and equity. Investments in rural and marginalized communities are essential to expand access to safe water and sanitation infrastructure. Policies must ensure affordability, protecting low-income households from excessive financial burdens. Strengthening community participation in decision-making enhances accountability and ensures that services reflect the needs of all populations. Integrating gender-sensitive approaches helps reduce the disproportionate burdens faced by women and girls, while recognizing indigenous knowledge and rights fosters inclusive governance. By tackling inequities at their root, societies can move toward achieving water justice and narrowing the health disparities that persist across communities.

Gender Dimensions of Water and Health

The relationship between water and health cannot be fully understood without recognizing the influence of gender. Across the world, gender roles, responsibilities, and inequalities shape how individuals access, use, and benefit from water services. Women and girls, in particular, bear disproportionate burdens related to water collection, sanitation, and hygiene, which directly affect their health, education, and economic opportunities. Men and boys also experience distinct challenges, but gender-based disparities are most evident in how women and girls are affected by water insecurity. Exploring these dimensions highlights the need for gender-sensitive approaches in water management to ensure equitable health outcomes.

One of the most visible gendered dimensions of water is the responsibility of water collection. In many rural and low-income contexts, women and girls are tasked with fetching water, often walking long distances and spending hours each day carrying heavy loads. This physically demanding labor has direct health consequences, including musculoskeletal injuries, fatigue, and risks associated with accidents or violence during collection. The time spent collecting water reduces opportunities for education and income-generating activities, perpetuating cycles of poverty and limiting social mobility. For girls, particularly, the burden of water collection can lead to school absenteeism, reducing long-term educational and health prospects.

Water, sanitation, and hygiene also intersect with gender in ways that profoundly affect women's and girls' health. Inadequate sanitation facilities compromise menstrual hygiene management, leading to infections, discomfort, and stigma. The lack of private, safe toilets in schools often results in absenteeism among adolescent girls, undermining their education and health. In healthcare facilities, insufficient water and sanitation put women at greater risk during childbirth, increasing maternal and neonatal morbidity and mortality. Women working in informal markets or agricultural labor also face occupational health risks when clean water is unavailable for washing or handling food.

Gender inequities are further reinforced by limited participation of women in water governance and decision-making. In many societies, water management institutions are male-dominated, and women's perspectives and needs are marginalized. This exclusion results in policies and infrastructure that fail to address the specific health vulnerabilities women and girls face. For instance, water points may be located without considering the safety of collection routes, or sanitation services may not provide privacy and security for women. By sidelining women's voices, governance structures perpetuate inequities that translate into health risks.

Men and boys also experience gendered health dimensions in relation to water, though in different ways. In some contexts, men are more exposed to occupational hazards associated with water-intensive industries, such as construction, fishing, or agriculture, where contaminated water or unsafe practices can lead to injury or disease. Social expectations around masculinity may also discourage men from engaging in household water and hygiene practices, which indirectly affects family health outcomes. Addressing gender dimensions therefore requires acknowledging the diverse needs and vulnerabilities of all genders.

Climate change and environmental stressors exacerbate gendered water-health disparities. Droughts, floods, and other water-related shocks often intensify the burden on women, who must travel further to collect water or manage household hygiene under increasingly difficult conditions. The physical and emotional strain of these responsibilities undermines mental health, creating hidden but significant gendered health impacts. Migration and displacement due to water scarcity can further expose women and girls to risks of violence and exploitation in insecure environments.

Addressing the gender dimensions of water and health requires deliberate action. Policies must prioritize gender equity in water service provision, ensuring that infrastructure design considers safety, privacy, and accessibility for women and girls. Efforts to improve sanitation in schools and healthcare facilities are essential for reducing health risks and supporting gender equality in education and maternal care. Empowering women to participate in decision-making about water governance enhances the inclusivity and effectiveness of policies, leading to more equitable health outcomes.

Gender-sensitive education and community engagement can also challenge harmful norms, encouraging men and boys to share responsibilities in water and hygiene practices.

By recognizing and addressing the gendered nature of water and health, societies can reduce disparities and strengthen overall resilience. Ensuring equitable access to safe water and sanitation is not only a public health priority but also a pathway to gender equality, social development, and sustainable well-being.

Urban-Rural Divide in Water Access

The urban-rural divide in water access remains one of the most persistent challenges in ensuring equitable health outcomes worldwide. Urban populations, particularly in developed regions, are more likely to benefit from piped water systems, centralized treatment facilities, and organized waste management. In contrast, rural communities often rely on decentralized, informal, or untreated water sources, exposing them to higher risks of contamination and scarcity. This divide reflects structural inequalities in infrastructure investment, governance, and resource allocation, resulting in stark differences in health outcomes between urban and rural populations.

Urban areas typically benefit from economies of scale that support investment in water infrastructure. Centralized water utilities can extend networks to millions of people, providing treated and regulated water that meets established quality standards. The availability of household connections also supports better sanitation and hygiene practices, reducing the prevalence of waterborne diseases. However, even within cities, disparities exist. Informal settlements and peri-urban neighborhoods are frequently excluded from municipal networks, leaving residents dependent on unsafe sources or expensive private vendors. This creates an urban paradox where proximity to modern infrastructure does not always guarantee access to safe water.

Rural communities face a different set of challenges rooted in geography and resource distribution. Sparse populations and greater distances make it difficult and costly to extend centralized water infrastructure to rural areas. Instead, many households rely on wells, boreholes, rivers, or rainwater harvesting, often without treatment or protection. These sources are vulnerable to contamination from human and animal waste, agricultural runoff, and industrial pollutants. As a result, rural populations face higher risks of diarrheal diseases, parasitic infections, and long-term exposure to harmful chemicals such as arsenic and fluoride. Limited infrastructure also constrains sanitation and hygiene, compounding health risks and reinforcing cycles of vulnerability.

The urban-rural divide is not only a matter of infrastructure but also governance and institutional capacity. Urban utilities often have stronger regulatory oversight, technical expertise, and financial resources compared to rural water committees or community-based organizations. Rural systems may depend on volunteer management, with limited ability to monitor water quality, maintain equipment, or secure financing for repairs. Governance gaps lead to inconsistent service provision and undermine trust in water systems, pushing rural households to rely on unsafe alternatives. Weak institutional support further limits opportunities to scale up innovative solutions that could bridge the divide.

Economic disparities exacerbate the divide. Rural households, often engaged in subsistence agriculture, have fewer resources to invest in safe water technologies such as filters or household treatment systems. Poverty constrains their ability to contribute to community infrastructure or pay for services when fees are required. At the same time, urban households benefit from subsidized utilities, creating inequities in how public funds are distributed. This imbalance leaves rural populations disproportionately burdened by water insecurity and its associated health impacts.

Climate change intensifies the urban-rural divide in water access. Rural communities dependent on rain-fed sources are more vulnerable to droughts, while floods can contaminate shallow wells and surface water. Urban areas, while also affected by climate extremes, often have more resilient infrastructure and emergency response systems in place. As water variability increases, rural populations are likely to experience heightened risks of scarcity and disease, widening health disparities further.

Addressing the urban-rural divide in water access requires targeted strategies that prioritize rural and underserved communities. Expanding decentralized systems such as solar-powered pumps, small-scale treatment plants, and community-managed distribution networks can improve access in areas where centralized infrastructure is not feasible. Investments in rural infrastructure must be accompanied by training, technical support, and financial mechanisms to ensure sustainability. Policies should also address inequities in public funding, ensuring that subsidies and resources are directed toward closing the rural gap rather than reinforcing urban advantages. Strengthening governance structures at the local level, with meaningful participation from communities, can improve accountability and build trust in water services.

Reducing the urban-rural divide is essential for advancing public health, social equity, and sustainable development. By addressing infrastructure, governance, and resource disparities, societies can ensure that both urban and rural populations benefit from safe, reliable, and affordable water services. Equalizing access is not only a matter of justice but also a prerequisite for reducing health disparities and building resilience in the face of future challenges.

Human Rights and the Right to Water and Health

The recognition of water as a human right underscores its essential role in ensuring health, dignity, and well-being. In 2010, the United Nations General Assembly explicitly recognized the human right to safe and clean drinking water and sanitation as fundamental to the realization of all human rights. This milestone affirmed that access to sufficient, safe, acceptable, physically accessible, and affordable water for personal and domestic use is indispensable for living a life with dignity. Closely tied to this recognition is the right to health, as water access directly influences disease prevention, nutrition, hygiene, and the ability of healthcare systems to function effectively.

The right to water is grounded in principles of equality and non-discrimination. It affirms that all individuals, regardless of gender, socioeconomic status, or geographic location, are entitled to adequate water for survival and health. Yet, in practice, billions of people continue to face water insecurity, with marginalized populations disproportionately excluded from safe and reliable services. This exclusion deepens health disparities, exposing vulnerable groups to waterborne diseases, malnutrition, and poor sanitation. The persistence of such inequities highlights the gap between legal recognition of rights and their realization on the ground.

The normative content of the right to water provides a framework for implementation. According to international human rights standards, water must be sufficient in quantity to meet basic needs for drinking, cooking, and hygiene. It must also be safe, free from contaminants that pose health risks, and acceptable in terms of taste, color, and cultural preferences. Accessibility requires that water be within safe physical reach and available without disproportionate effort or risk. Affordability ensures that the cost of water does not compromise the ability of households to secure other essential needs. These criteria establish benchmarks against which governments and institutions can be held accountable for ensuring universal access.

The right to health is inseparable from the right to water. Safe water and adequate sanitation are foundational to preventing infectious diseases such as cholera, dysentery, and typhoid. They also play a role in reducing maternal and child mortality by supporting safe childbirth and child development. Access to clean water enables proper hygiene in healthcare facilities, ensuring that medical procedures do not transmit infections. Furthermore, the availability of safe water underpins nutrition by supporting agriculture and food safety, linking water access directly to broader determinants of health. Without adequate water, the right to health cannot be realized.

Governments bear the primary responsibility for fulfilling the right to water and health. This obligation requires them to respect, protect, and fulfill these rights by refraining from interfering with access, regulating private actors, and taking proactive measures to expand services. Public investment in infrastructure, enforcement of water quality standards, and targeted support for vulnerable communities are key to meeting these obligations. At the same time, international cooperation plays a crucial role, as many countries lack the financial or technical resources to ensure universal access on their own. Global solidarity, through funding, technology transfer, and capacity-building, is essential to advancing these rights.

Challenges to realizing the right to water and health persist in many regions. Climate change threatens the availability and reliability of water sources, while pollution and overextraction compromise safety and sustainability. Conflicts and displacement often disrupt water services, leaving populations dependent on unsafe alternatives. Privatization of water services, if not carefully regulated, can lead to affordability barriers that violate human rights principles. These challenges underscore the need for robust governance frameworks that place human rights at the center of water and health policies.

Civil society and community participation are vital in advancing these rights. Grassroots movements and advocacy organizations play a critical role in holding governments accountable, raising awareness of inequities, and empowering marginalized groups to demand their entitlements. Participation enhances the legitimacy and effectiveness of water governance, ensuring that policies reflect the needs and realities of diverse populations. By embedding human rights principles into water management, societies can create inclusive systems that prioritize dignity, equity, and health for all.

The recognition of water and health as human rights establishes both a moral and legal imperative for action. Ensuring access to safe, sufficient, and affordable water is not merely a development goal but a fundamental entitlement that underpins life and health. By upholding these rights, governments and societies affirm the principle that health and well-being should not be determined by geography, wealth, or social status, but guaranteed for every individual.

Chapter 9: Governance, Policy, and Integrated Approaches

The intersection of water and health demands governance systems and policies that move beyond sectoral boundaries. Effective governance ensures that water resources are managed sustainably, equitably, and in ways that prioritize public health. Policies linking water and health establish standards, allocate resources, and provide frameworks for collaboration across institutions and sectors. Integrated approaches recognize that water challenges are interconnected with sanitation, food systems, climate resilience, and social equity, requiring coordination among diverse stakeholders. This chapter explores how governance, policy, and integrated strategies shape water and health outcomes, emphasizing the importance of accountability, inclusion, and long-term sustainability.

Global Frameworks and Institutional Architectures

The governance of water and health is shaped not only by national policies but also by global frameworks and institutional architectures that establish norms, provide guidance, and facilitate cooperation. These frameworks are critical in addressing transboundary water challenges, mobilizing resources, and promoting equity in access to safe water and sanitation. They also play a central role in integrating water security into broader global agendas such as health, human rights, and sustainable development. Examining these global structures reveals how international norms and institutions shape the pursuit of safe water and better health outcomes worldwide.

One of the most influential global frameworks is the Sustainable Development Goals (SDGs), adopted by the United Nations in 2015. Goal 6 explicitly calls for ensuring availability and sustainable management of water and sanitation for all, while other goals, such as those on health (Goal 3), climate action (Goal 13), and inequality (Goal 10), intersect with water-related targets. The SDGs recognize that water security is integral to achieving health, equity, and environmental sustainability. Their universal and time-bound targets provide benchmarks for countries to measure progress and identify gaps, while the emphasis on leaving no one behind highlights equity as a guiding principle.

The WHO plays a central role in linking water governance with health outcomes. Through its normative guidance, technical assistance, and monitoring initiatives, WHO provides standards and protocols for water safety and quality. For instance, the Guidelines for Drinking-water Quality establish international benchmarks for safe water, shaping national regulations and informing infrastructure development. WHO also leads efforts in WASH in healthcare facilities, recognizing their role in infection prevention and control. By integrating water considerations into public health strategies, WHO ensures that water and health are addressed as inseparable priorities.

The United Nations Children's Fund (UNICEF) complements WHO's role by focusing on access to water and sanitation for children and communities. Together, WHO and UNICEF co-lead the Joint Monitoring Programme (JMP), which provides global data on WASH access. This monitoring system is essential for tracking progress toward the SDGs and identifying inequities in access across regions and populations. Reliable global data strengthens accountability, enabling governments and international organizations to target interventions where they are most needed. It also highlights persistent gaps in rural, marginalized, and conflict-affected areas, emphasizing the urgency of action.

Beyond UN agencies, international financial institutions such as the World Bank and regional development banks are crucial actors in the global institutional architecture. They provide loans, grants, and technical assistance for water infrastructure and management projects. Their influence extends beyond financing, as they shape policy directions by encouraging reforms in governance, pricing, and service delivery. While these institutions have supported significant improvements in water access, their emphasis on cost recovery and private sector participation has sometimes raised concerns about affordability and equity. Balancing efficiency and inclusivity remains a key challenge in aligning financial mechanisms with global rights-based frameworks.

Transboundary water governance adds another dimension to global frameworks. Rivers, lakes, and aquifers that cross national borders require cooperative management to prevent conflicts and ensure equitable use. Frameworks such as the UN Watercourses Convention and the UNECE Water Convention establish principles for cooperation, information sharing, and dispute resolution. These conventions are important for protecting ecosystems and human health in regions where shared resources are vital for drinking water, agriculture, and energy. However, the effectiveness of transboundary governance depends on political will, institutional capacity, and the ability to balance national interests with collective health and sustainability goals.

Global health and humanitarian organizations also play significant roles. Agencies such as the International Committee of the Red Cross and non-governmental organizations like WaterAid or Médecins Sans Frontières provide emergency water and sanitation services in conflict zones, refugee camps, and disaster-affected regions. Their interventions prevent disease outbreaks and protect vulnerable populations when state systems collapse. These organizations contribute not only through service delivery but also by advocating for stronger commitments to the human right to water and health at global forums.

The institutional architecture also includes multi-stakeholder partnerships that bridge governments, civil society, and the private sector. Initiatives such as Sanitation and Water for All (SWA) provide platforms for dialogue, accountability, and resource mobilization. These partnerships align diverse actors toward common goals, fostering collective action to address persistent gaps in access and health outcomes. By bringing together local and global perspectives, they enhance coordination and ensure that global commitments translate into local impact.

Despite the progress made, challenges remain in strengthening global frameworks and institutional architectures. Fragmentation among international organizations can lead to overlapping mandates and inefficiencies. Limited resources and uneven political commitment hinder the implementation of ambitious global goals. Moreover, global frameworks often face difficulties in ensuring accountability at the national level, where political, economic, and social factors influence the pace of progress. Bridging these gaps requires stronger coordination among international institutions, clearer division of responsibilities, and enhanced support for capacity-building at the country level.

Global frameworks and institutional architectures provide a vital foundation for addressing the nexus of water and health. By establishing norms, mobilizing resources, and fostering cooperation, they guide national and local efforts toward universal access and health equity. As climate change, population growth, and urbanization intensify pressures on water systems, the role of these global structures will become even more important. Strengthening their coherence, inclusivity, and accountability is essential to ensuring that safe water and health are recognized not only as development goals but also as fundamental rights for all.

National Policies Linking Water and Health

National policies are critical in translating global frameworks and principles into concrete actions that ensure safe, sufficient, and equitable access to water and health services. These policies establish the legal, institutional, and financial foundations for addressing water-related health risks, while also shaping how governments allocate resources and prioritize interventions. Effective policies bridge the gap between water management and health outcomes, fostering cross-sectoral collaboration that strengthens both systems.

A fundamental element of national policies linking water and health is the establishment of water quality standards. Governments define permissible levels of microbial and chemical contaminants, drawing on international guidelines such as those from the World Health Organization. These standards guide utilities, regulators, and public health agencies in monitoring and enforcement, ensuring that drinking water is safe for consumption. By integrating these standards into national legal frameworks, countries provide accountability mechanisms that protect populations from both acute and chronic waterborne health risks.

Sanitation and hygiene policies complement water supply regulations by reducing exposure to pathogens and promoting healthier environments. Many governments adopt integrated WASH strategies that align health and water priorities. These policies often target critical settings such as schools and healthcare facilities, where inadequate WASH services increase vulnerability to infections. By mandating minimum service standards and directing funding to underserved areas, national policies reduce disease transmission and enhance public health resilience.

Another crucial dimension is the integration of water management into health planning. National health policies increasingly recognize the importance of addressing environmental determinants of health, including water safety. This integration takes the form of water safety plans, which systematically assess and manage risks across the entire water supply chain, from source protection to household consumption. By embedding water safety planning into health strategies, governments create preventive systems that reduce the incidence of disease outbreaks linked to water contamination.

National disaster risk reduction and climate adaptation policies also link water and health. Governments are developing strategies to anticipate and mitigate the health impacts of droughts, floods, and waterborne disease outbreaks exacerbated by climate change. These policies often prioritize resilient infrastructure, early warning systems, and emergency response mechanisms. Health ministries and water authorities collaborate to ensure that water services remain operational during crises, safeguarding essential health functions and reducing vulnerability among at-risk populations.

Equity is a defining principle of national policies that link water and health. Governments must ensure that policies address disparities in access across urban and rural populations, as well as among marginalized groups. Subsidies, targeted investments, and inclusive governance mechanisms help bridge inequalities and advance the human right to water and health. Policies that prioritize gender-sensitive approaches, such as improving sanitation for women and girls or addressing the disproportionate burdens of water collection, strengthen social equity alongside health outcomes.

Financing and institutional arrangements form the backbone of policy implementation. National policies establish funding mechanisms, such as water tariffs, taxes, and subsidies, to sustain infrastructure and services. They also define institutional roles, clarifying the responsibilities of water utilities, health ministries, environmental regulators, and local governments. Effective coordination between these actors ensures that policies are implemented consistently and that water and health priorities are aligned. In many cases, interministerial committees or task forces are created to oversee integrated approaches, breaking down silos between sectors.

Finally, monitoring and accountability systems are essential components of national policies linking water and health. Governments establish surveillance systems to track waterborne diseases, monitor water quality, and assess service coverage. Data collection and reporting not only enable policymakers to evaluate progress but also provide transparency to the public. By embedding monitoring into policy frameworks, governments can adjust strategies to respond to emerging risks and ensure continuous improvement.

National policies serve as the foundation for securing the water-health nexus. By setting standards, integrating planning, promoting equity, and strengthening institutions, these policies create environments where safe water and public health reinforce one another. Their success depends on strong governance, sustained investment, and inclusive implementation that prioritizes the well-being of all populations.

Financing Water and Health Interventions

Financing is a cornerstone of effective water and health interventions. Without adequate and sustainable funding, even well-designed policies and infrastructure plans cannot deliver lasting improvements in public health. Financing water and health interventions involves mobilizing resources, structuring cost recovery mechanisms, and ensuring equitable distribution of funds to reach vulnerable populations. Governments, international organizations, financial institutions, and communities all play a role in creating systems that support access to safe water, sanitation, and health services.

Public investment is the foundation of financing water and health. Governments allocate resources to build and maintain infrastructure, regulate water quality, and support public health programs. National budgets often provide funding for rural water supply, urban sanitation networks, and disease prevention campaigns. However, competing demands on public finances can limit the scale of investment, particularly in low- and middle-income countries. In these contexts, prioritization is crucial. Allocating funds to preventive measures such as safe water systems and hygiene promotion often yields greater long-term health and economic benefits than focusing solely on curative health services.

International development assistance is another vital source of financing. Multilateral agencies such as the World Bank, regional development banks, and United Nations programs provide loans, grants, and technical assistance for large-scale water and health projects. Bilateral aid from donor governments also supports infrastructure development, capacity-building, and emergency responses. These resources are particularly important for countries with limited fiscal capacity, enabling them to address structural inequities in water and health access. However, reliance on external financing can create vulnerabilities if projects are not aligned with national priorities or if funding is inconsistent. Strong governance is therefore needed to ensure that international financing complements, rather than substitutes, domestic efforts.

Private sector participation adds another layer of financing mechanisms. Public-private partnerships (PPPs) are often used to expand water infrastructure, bring in technical expertise, and improve efficiency. Private actors may provide capital for projects such as water treatment plants, distribution networks, or sanitation services, with cost recovery through tariffs or service fees. While PPPs can mobilize additional resources, they must be carefully regulated to safeguard affordability and equity. Without oversight, privatization risks excluding low-income households that cannot afford market-based pricing. Transparent contracts, subsidies for vulnerable groups, and clear accountability frameworks are essential to ensure that private sector involvement supports public health objectives.

Innovative financing approaches are emerging to address the persistent funding gap in water and health. Blended finance mechanisms combine public and private capital to de-risk investments in underserved areas. Social impact bonds and results-based financing tie funding to measurable health outcomes, incentivizing efficiency and accountability. Climate finance, including funds from mechanisms such as the Green Climate Fund, increasingly supports water interventions that build resilience to climate-related health risks. By linking financing to long-term sustainability and health impacts, these approaches broaden the scope of funding opportunities.

Cost recovery through user fees remains a central but controversial component of financing. Tariffs on water services help cover operation and maintenance costs, ensuring the sustainability of systems. However, affordability is a critical concern. Poor households often spend a larger share of their income on water, and high tariffs can exacerbate inequities. Progressive pricing structures, lifeline tariffs for basic consumption, and targeted subsidies are tools that balance cost recovery with equity. Effective financing frameworks must therefore ensure that cost recovery does not undermine the right to water and health.

Community financing also plays a role, particularly in rural and decentralized systems. Local contributions, whether monetary or in-kind labor, support the construction and maintenance of small-scale water systems. These mechanisms foster ownership and accountability, increasing the likelihood of long-term sustainability. However, community financing must be supplemented by external support to provide technical expertise and cover costs beyond local capacity. Relying solely on community resources risks perpetuating inequities, as poorer communities are less able to mobilize sufficient funds.

Ultimately, financing water and health interventions requires a mix of sources and mechanisms tailored to national contexts. Public investment, international aid, private participation, innovative tools, and community contributions all have roles to play. The challenge lies in balancing sustainability, efficiency, and equity. Ensuring that resources reach the most vulnerable populations is paramount, as inequitable financing structures can perpetuate disparities in health outcomes. By building inclusive, transparent, and resilient financing systems, countries can secure the resources needed to guarantee safe water and health for all.

Cross-Sectoral Collaboration and Integrated Governance

The intersection of water and health challenges requires solutions that cut across traditional sectoral boundaries. Water systems influence public health, agriculture, energy, and the environment, making siloed approaches inadequate for addressing complex risks. Cross-sectoral collaboration and integrated governance provide a framework for coordinating policies, aligning investments, and ensuring that water and health priorities are mutually reinforcing. By fostering cooperation among diverse stakeholders, governments and institutions can build more resilient and inclusive systems.

Cross-sectoral collaboration begins with the recognition that water and health outcomes are shaped by multiple determinants. Ministries of water, health, agriculture, environment, and finance often have overlapping mandates, yet historically they have operated independently. This fragmentation creates gaps in service delivery, inefficiencies in resource allocation, and missed opportunities for prevention. Integrated governance addresses these challenges by creating mechanisms for coordination, whether through interministerial committees, national task forces, or joint planning frameworks. Such mechanisms ensure that policies are harmonized and that health considerations are embedded in water management decisions.

At the national level, integrated governance promotes alignment between health and water policies. For example, water safety plans developed by utilities can be coordinated with disease surveillance systems overseen by health ministries. This integration allows for early detection of waterborne outbreaks and rapid response to contamination events. Similarly, sanitation programs can be linked with nutrition initiatives to address the combined risks of malnutrition and poor hygiene. By aligning sectoral policies, governments can achieve synergies that enhance efficiency and improve health outcomes.

Local governance structures also play a vital role in cross-sectoral collaboration. Municipalities and community organizations are often responsible for implementing water and health services, making coordination essential at the grassroots level. Participatory governance models that involve local stakeholders, including civil society and user associations, strengthen accountability and ensure that services are responsive to community needs. Collaboration at the local level is especially important in rural and underserved areas, where integrated solutions can address multiple vulnerabilities simultaneously.

Internationally, integrated governance is supported by frameworks that encourage multi-sectoral approaches. The Sustainable Development Goals emphasize the interconnectedness of water, health, and other priorities, urging countries to adopt holistic strategies. Partnerships such as Sanitation and Water for All provide platforms for governments, civil society, and donors to align their efforts. These initiatives highlight the importance of shared accountability and collective action in achieving global targets.

Financing mechanisms benefit from cross-sectoral collaboration by pooling resources and aligning investments. For instance, climate adaptation funds can support projects that enhance both water security and public health resilience. Agricultural programs that promote efficient irrigation can also contribute to safe water access by reducing contamination risks. Integrated financing approaches recognize the co-benefits of interventions across sectors, maximizing the impact of limited resources.

Challenges to integrated governance persist, including institutional inertia, competing priorities, and limited technical capacity. Ministries may resist ceding authority, while fragmented funding streams reinforce siloed approaches. Overcoming these barriers requires political commitment, capacity-building, and clear incentives for collaboration. Developing shared performance indicators across sectors can strengthen accountability and encourage cooperation. Training programs that build interdisciplinary expertise also help bridge gaps between water and health professionals.

Cross-sectoral collaboration and integrated governance are not optional but essential for addressing the water-health nexus in an era of growing complexity. By aligning policies, institutions, and resources, governments can create systems that are more efficient, equitable, and resilient. These approaches ensure that safe water and public health are not treated as separate issues but as interdependent priorities that require collective responsibility and coordinated action.

Conclusion

Water is inseparable from human health, shaping outcomes that range from individual well-being to the resilience of societies. Throughout this book, the multiple pathways through which water affects health have been explored, highlighting both the direct and indirect consequences of water quality, availability, and governance. From ensuring physiological needs and preventing disease to supporting sanitation, food security, and healthcare delivery, water underpins nearly every dimension of public health. Understanding these interconnections is essential for designing policies and interventions that protect populations and promote equity.

The challenges identified are complex and multifaceted. Microbial and chemical contaminants continue to threaten drinking water safety, while inadequate sanitation and hygiene perpetuate cycles of disease transmission. Vector-borne and parasitic infections remain tied to poor water management, especially in areas lacking infrastructure. Water scarcity contributes to malnutrition and undermines child development, while climate change intensifies risks by disrupting supplies and amplifying the frequency of extreme weather events. These pressures are compounded by socioeconomic inequities, with vulnerable populations disproportionately exposed to unsafe water and its health impacts.

At the same time, the opportunities for progress are clear. Strengthening governance, improving infrastructure, and embedding health priorities into water policies can significantly reduce preventable diseases and enhance resilience. Integrating health considerations into water management ensures that interventions address not only technical challenges but also the broader determinants of health. Financing models that balance cost recovery with equity can sustain infrastructure while protecting the most vulnerable. Community participation and inclusive governance amplify these efforts by ensuring that services reflect diverse needs and that populations are active partners in maintaining health security.

The role of global and national frameworks is central in driving progress. International agendas such as the Sustainable Development Goals provide a unifying vision, while institutions like the World Health Organization and UNICEF set standards and track progress. National governments translate these commitments into policies that establish legal standards, allocate resources, and ensure accountability. Cross-sectoral collaboration enhances these efforts by aligning water, health, environmental, and financial priorities. Together, these layers of governance form the architecture needed to safeguard health through water security.

Looking ahead, the importance of resilience cannot be overstated. Climate change, rapid urbanization, and population growth will continue to strain water systems and test the capacity of health infrastructures. Building resilience requires adaptive governance that evolves with emerging risks, innovative technologies that improve monitoring and service delivery, and sustainable financing that ensures long-term functionality. Equally important is the commitment to equity, ensuring that progress does not leave behind rural communities, informal settlements, or marginalized groups who face the highest burdens of water-related health risks.

Water and health are not separate policy domains but intertwined priorities that demand integrated solutions. By addressing inequities, strengthening governance, and fostering collaboration across sectors, societies can create systems that ensure universal access to safe, sufficient, and affordable water. Such systems are not only a safeguard against disease but also a foundation for human dignity, social development, and environmental sustainability. The pursuit of health through water security is, ultimately, a pursuit of justice and resilience—a recognition that the right to water and the right to health are fundamental and inseparable.

www.ingramcontent.com/pod-product-compliance
Lightning Source LLC
Chambersburg PA
CBHW071606200326

41519CB00021BB/6896